HOW TO GET A GREAT JOB IN 90 DAYS OR LESS

JOE CARROLL
SPHR, CMF

Copyright 2010 by Joseph Kane Carroll

All rights reserved; no part of this publication may be reproduced, stored in a retrieval system, or transmitted, in any form or by any means, electronic, mechanical, photocopying, recording, or otherwise, without the prior written permission of Joseph Kane Carroll.

Manufactured in the United States of America

ISBN: 0-9664386-4-7
ISBN-13: 9780966438642
Library of Congress Control Number: 2010936749

To request permission for reproduction or inquire about career coaching or speaking engagements, contact:

Email Joe Carroll at Joekane@aol.com
Web site: www.career-coach-now.com

CONTENTS

Acknowledgments   v

Introduction   vii

1. Find Your Passion: Getting the Gold Requires a Little Digging   1

2. Your Preferences Will Keep You on the Right Path   13

3. Your Talent is the Key to Unlocking Your Destiny   21

4. Fitness: Your Choice—It Takes a Lean Horse to Stay in the Race   33

5. Ten Job Secrets They Never Taught You in College   43

6. Master the Philosophy of Self-fulfillment   53

7. The Eight Things You Need to Know About Managing Your Career   63

8. Getting Fired Can Be a Blessing in Disguise   73

9. Stop Wasting Your Time   79

10. You are the Product   85

11.	How to Take the Work Out of Networking	95
12.	Smile, Dial and Make the Phone Your Best Friend	107
13.	Interviewing is Selling and You are the Merchandise	131
14.	How to Clean Your Life with a New Broom	143
15.	Trust Your Hunches and Go with Your Instincts	149
16.	Your Blueprint for Life Requires a Few Goals	155

ACKNOWLEDGMENTS

This book developed over many years as a result of my interests in career coaching, executive recruiting, outplacement, public speaking, and hunting for new job opportunities.

I know what it is like to be unemployed and to experience the fear of uncertainty, not knowing when the next paycheck would be forthcoming. But every night has a new dawn with bright beginnings. I also experienced the excitement and euphoria associated with job offers. It is through the tough times and the good times that I have relied on my family and friends. They have all been my positive sphere of influence.

I want to thank those people who provided me with great insight, friendship, love, and honesty over the years. All of them had an impact on the writing of this book. They include my wife, Carol Ann, my son, Joe, my sister, Diane, my brothers, Terry and Bobby, and three of my trusted friends for many years: Larry Lee, Ronnie Smolinsky, and Richie Waxman.

INTRODUCTION

"Only passions, great passions, can elevate the soul to great things."

- Denis Diderot

Why ninety days to get a great job? Why not six months or a year? Do you actually have six months or a year to find new employment? Most people don't have this luxury. Getting a job is like consultative selling. You're developing a relationship with someone who can either refer you or hire you. It's that simple. Developing relationships takes a little time. If you were fired from your job tomorrow, how long would it take you to find a new job? I have heard of people who have been out of work for over two years!

So is this book just for the unemployed? Absolutely not! However, if you are unemployed, this book should become your road map to a new job. If you are still working, this book will provide invaluable tips on what you can do before you leave or get booted from your job. It's just a matter of time before you separate from your current employer. Most people, these days, will not remain with the same employer long term. This book is particularly useful for professionals, managers, and executives. These are the people who typically rely on their networks to get information, leads, and future job opportunities. Other people just starting out their careers can also glean a lot from this book and put it to future use.

There are hundreds of books available on job search strategies. Go to any book store and you will probably see fifty to one hundred books on the subject. I've read many of them. The missing link between a successful job search and career management is self-fulfillment. Self-fulfillment is driven, in part, by your passions, talents, preferences, and purpose in life. You should not separate your job and your life's purpose. If you do, it can easily become a pathway to disappointment. Later I discuss in some detail how to master the philosophy of self-fulfillment.

This book goes beyond successful job hunting. It is not just about your next employer. The fact is, over the course of a lifetime, you may have ten, twenty, or more different employers. You may even have three to five or more different careers until you finally figure out exactly what you want to do with your life. Time is precious. I believe ninety days establishes a sense of urgency.

This book is not just about landing a great job. It is about your callings. Callings go beyond occupations, professions, or careers. It is an inner urge to pursue something meaningful in life. When you can align your inner urge to your field of choice, you are definitely going in the right direction.

I am a certified expert on career management. I have developed strategies and a philosophy that suggests a strong connection between your passion, preferences, purpose in life, and your career of choice. These connections need to be in alignment. If they don't align, you will be out of balance. You will not be in sync. Therefore, you will not reach your full potential.

I am about to share with you in this book the blueprint for accomplishing your highest potential in three short months. Some of the secrets may result in an epiphany, revelation, or catalyst for change in your life. However, my philosophy is not for everyone. Plato did not believe everything that Socrates tried to teach him. And contrary to popular belief, great minds do not often think alike. However, here is one brilliant quote that could have been written by Plato or Socrates (historians simply do not know):

"The unexamined life is not worth living."

It is not important who said it. It is important to do it. I need you to examine your life. You are here on this place we call earth to get your act together. It is in your interest to be the best that you can be. A good chunk of this book will seek to get you to examine your life in great detail because your life is worth living!

This book is not for those who seek to live an average life. I am really not interested in average. I am interested in **getting average people to become above-average people.** I am interested in achieving powerful results. This book is not for those who refuse to stretch their minds to a new level. I have absolutely nothing against people who want to live an average life. They are no better than me and I am no better than them. I am not a judge.

My goal is for you to achieve your dreams and become the person you were meant to be. If wealth is a by-product of your dreams—so be it. Money is not evil. My concern is that many people go on autopilot in life. They either abandon or forget why they are here, and their dreams become a blur as the years race by.

Part of your ninety-day job search is to understand the benefits of living a no-regrets life. I don't offer you the secrets to longevity or the fountain of youth. I don't guarantee that you will live to be ninety years old. Your genetics has a lot to do with your life span. However, it will provide you with a blueprint for living a no-regrets life. Depending on how long you will work during your lifetime, you will probably spend forty to fifty years carving out a living. The unfortunate truth is that the majority of you will not enjoy your work. My question is this: how can someone go through fifty years of working and absolutely hate what he or she does? It almost defies logic. You will spend a lifetime pursuing a paycheck while your life's purpose is going bankrupt. What an incredible waste of energy and happiness! It doesn't have to be that way.

It took me many years to develop my strategies and philosophy. I was fortunate enough to discover my passion during my teen years. I listened to my inner voice. However, it took me a long time to figure out how to activate my passions. It's one thing to be passionate. It's quite another to put your passions in action. One of the secrets is to focus on your dreams and start making decisions. Making a decision can bring emeralds to your soul. Making any kind of decision and taking action is moving forward with the great stream of life.

"Inaction breeds doubt and fear. Action breeds confidence and courage. If you want to conquer fear, do not sit home and think about it. Go out and get busy."

- Dale Carnegie

The well-spent life is not an accident. It requires diligence, perseverance, and a restless desire to pursue those outcomes propelled by your dreams, passions, and purpose in life. It is the kind of stuff that energizes people, creates miracles, accumulates wealth, builds great companies, conquers disease, and puts men on the moon and beyond. People need to be in pursuit of their passions to maximize success. Is success the end game?

When you pursue your calling in life, it starts to produce a state of happiness and fulfillment which is really the definition of true success. Most people never think twice about their purpose or passion. People can be quite successful and never give an ounce of thought to the question: why am I here? Og Mandino once said, "I am here for a purpose, and that purpose is to grow into a mountain, not to shrink to a grain of sand. Henceforth will I apply *all* my efforts to become the highest mountain of all, and I will strain my potential until it cries for mercy." The human race is a grand mosaic from Mozart to candlestick makers. All can choose to be utterly happy or miserable or somewhere in between. The choice is yours.

Regardless of your station in life, the worst-case scenario is to be at death's door and suddenly realize you did not fulfill your goals or purpose in life. It's called regrets. It surfaces out of your gut and there is nothing you can do about it in your final moments in life. What exactly happens when you die? Have you ever been with someone when he or she died? I have. When some people die, they look towards the heavens. There may be a ceiling, but they are looking into the universe. Their eyes have the look of awe. Few people can imagine what it is like to look upon the face of God. There is nothing to fear. Helen Keller once said, "Death is no more than passing from one room into another. But there's a difference for me, you know, because in that other room I shall be able to see." Helen Keller was saying that in the next life, her soul would have perfect vision. She may have been blind, but yet she sees. Our purpose for being here can be found in our genetic code, which influences the mind.

If we assume that you have a purpose for being here, then clearly we need to try and figure out what that purpose is. I have found that the subconscious often communicates when you least expect it. Sometimes we refer to it as a sixth sense, intuition, or extrasensory perception. A message could come during a dream, in the shower, driving a car, or just plain daydreaming. How often have we heard it said: "I have a feeling about this," "Go with your gut," or "Let your conscience be your guide"? Sometimes you wake up in the middle of the night with a clear message. My advice is to immediately write it down because you will most likely forget it once you go back to sleep. Keep a notepad on your nightstand for this purpose. Regardless of your mission on earth, your ultimate goal is to fulfill your life's purpose. Getting a handle on your purpose is difficult, but not impossible. You need to accomplish this now or at least within the next ninety days. Your future may depend on it!

The best advice I can give you on this subject is to be more receptive when you hear your internal voice communicating with you. Don't ignore it. Your calling in life will often be revealed to you through your inner mind.

Science and the idea of a sixth sense are not likely to be a subject of discussion within the great halls of science. I think there is room for both in a universe filled with some one hundred billion galaxies, each containing an innumerable number of stars and planets. Science tells us the universe began with a big bang 13.7 billion years ago. *Homo sapiens* (man) did not come on the scene until approximately three to four hundred thousand years ago. How did we get smart enough to build the Sphinx when we were still running around in animal skins and could barely read and write? Did we get a little help from lost civilizations? Scientists today still have not been able to answer that question. It's a complete and total mystery.

It was only forty years ago that Commander Neil Armstrong became the first man on the moon. So we are the new kids on the block in the big scheme of things. I think that requires a certain amount of humility and awe. What is the connection between the big bang, God, lost civilizations, and getting a new job in ninety days or less? In a word: everything. Let's start with this first premise: humility is an asset, and everything that goes around comes around.

My view is that we came into this world for a reason. From the moment of conception, we are on a quest to achieve something. This is why you cannot separate your career from your purpose in life. This place called earth is a training camp, and work is a big part of that training. It is generally not a good idea to spend only 10 percent of your time on life goals and the other 90 percent on job goals. Your career is interwoven with your purpose. It's actually a miracle that you are here in the first place given the army of sperm cells in your mother's womb that raced to the finish line during procreation. There could be only one winner in this chariot race. In one sense, we are all living miracles.

As the years race by, we sometimes sense that the outcomes are disappointing. We can't go back in time. Time travel is not possible yet. We can't undo what we did. This is not to say that we are perfect. All of us have flaws that surface, in one way or another. The key is to learn, correct, adjust, and start over. Many people will expire after living a life filled with utter regret. It doesn't have to be that way. It's one of the reasons I'm writing this book. Getting to seventy and beyond happens in a flash. We are here for one tiny speck in time. It's time to change gears.

A huge part of the problem is that we were never taught to align our purpose, passion, and preferences in life to our chosen vocation. We were never taught how to listen to our inner voice. Yes, many schools have career counselors, but they do not get into discussions about purpose and passion. For most of them, it comes down to interpreting a psychological test, forming conclusions, and telling the student where they think he or she should be going. The problem is that it is the student that needs to come to a conclusion and not the counselor advising the student.

Thus, we can spend a lifetime in an occupation that is totally out of alignment with our true purpose or preferences. What an incredible waste of energy! This can lead to stress, job hopping, termination, family squabbles, divorce, and lack of fulfillment. If, for example, one of your preferences is autonomy, and you have a boss who is micromanaging you, your level of job satisfaction is probably going to be really low. High schools and colleges need to start offering courses that help students better prepare for their careers and to ensure the chosen field is in alignment with their purpose and goals in life. This makes sense to me.

Hopefully, you're getting a sense that I feel pretty passionate about some things. Passion is good. Feelings are great. Many people are trained to be rational thinkers. They believe their emotions should not come into the equation. Emotions, I believe, are at the core of your being. You need to trust them and go with the flow. This book is designed to help you alter your outcomes in life in a passionate way. It does not matter how old you are or what you do for a living. It does not matter what your religion is or what color your skin might be. You might be a student in high school or college or perhaps a homemaker or retiree. It is never too late to turn a page and go forward in a new direction. It is simply a matter of taking a position and stating, "This is the day I will be changing my life forever." There is a strategy for making this happen. You can trust me on this. The strategy is described in this book. It is a strategy for maximizing your full potential.

It was Rene Descartes that once said, "It is not enough to have a good mind; the main thing is to use it well." What a novel idea to use the mind well. What a novel idea! Descartes developed his amazing philosophy during the 1600s. He actually developed a solid philosophy that had practical applications. The man was way ahead of his time. However, he could not deal with the cold weather and died of pneumonia at the age of fifty-four. He was persuaded to go to Sweden to teach philosophy to the queen of Sweden. Apparently, he was required to arise at five o'clock in the morning for his classes. He quickly contracted pneumonia and died shortly thereafter. Is there a message here about common sense?

Life can be about sacrifice and hard work. If you want to make it in this world, it can take some work and some sacrifice. Nothing comes easy in this world. When you were born, it was not an easy thing for your mother to move you from her womb to the outer world. There was some pain in the process. We were all born with this idea of pain and struggle. If you can connect your passion with your calling in life, I doubt for one moment that you will consider what you are doing is hard work. It will be a labor of love.

The universe is an ocean of unlimited questions. We will have questions until we die. That, my friend, is for certain.

Indeed, when we die, we will be questioning whether or not we achieved our life's purpose. Will we have any regrets? If we had more time, would we do something different?

The questions are endless. Why do some people win and others lose? How come some people are happy and others are absolutely miserable? Why do some people get angry and lose total control while others seem to coast and enjoy the ride? Why is it that 80 percent of the world's population can be classified as poor? Why is it that the top 20 percent owns 80 percent of all wealth in the United States? Why are some people rich and others poor? Are we destined to be boxed into some form of income level regardless of our efforts, education, hard work, and station in life? Who defines the dimensions, possibilities, and final outcomes? Is there life after death or is this the end of the ride? Who gets to be buried in a pine box instead of a steel vault? Why would one decide to scatter his or her ashes across the Potomac River or some mountaintop?

These questions, on one level, may seem deep and complex. Some of the questions may suggest that this book is about economics, philosophy, or religion. While we talk about all of these elements, the truth is this book addresses a totally different perspective on life and work. Why do some people win and others lose? Is it really about winning and losing? Some suggest we should live in the present for tomorrow may never come. There certainly is some truth with that concept.

This book, on the other hand, encourages you to live somewhat on the edge. The main goal is to find a job within three short months. That means taking some risks. I dare you to take risks. Life was a risk when you squeezed out of your mother's womb. It sure was a lot more warm and cozy inside. I suggest that you use your emotions to live life and balance it with rock-solid standards to get the most out of life. The bottom line is that there is an art and a science to living the good life to maximize your time on earth. I believe you can figure it out in ninety days. There are principles and techniques that can help you achieve a well-spent life. My message remains clear. You have a calling, and my advice is to figure out your calling in ninety days and get your career on track. Your career will consume most of your life. You need to be on the right track. You cannot afford to spend a lifetime on the wrong side of the road.

Let's talk briefly about money. Money is not the root of all evil. I believe in the laws of supply and demand. I believe that free enterprise is one of the things that made the United States the best and most prosperous country in the world. We are also the most generous country in the world. There are lots of books that will tell you how to accumulate wealth. I don't believe that the pursuit of money is the right motivator. Money is simply a by-product of our efforts in life. If you work, you get paid. Hard work does not necessarily translate into big bucks. Any construction worker knows that.

The real questions are: What will you do, how much will you earn, and, more importantly, will you be happy and fulfilled? If you find that you are in the 80 percent group that is currently just getting by, how do you get into the 20 percent group that is enjoying the fruits of their labor? Let me be clear: I have nothing against the 80 percent group. People make choices. My choice is to get into the 20 percent group. You don't need to have a high IQ to accumulate wealth. Indeed, intelligence has very little to do with wealth and may even be a detriment to acquiring wealth. According to a study by Ohio State University, people with a higher IQ do not do well long term on the prosperity front. In fact, people who are more in the middle of the intelligent quotient tend to do better over time.

Financial security is an important factor for all of us. The sad truth is that many of us live beyond our means. Over 40 percent of Americans spend more than they earn. Credit card debt for the average American is $9,000 or more. The average American has thirteen credit cards! The decisions we make in life today will obviously shape and mold our destiny. You are the chief architect of your economic destiny. This book is about your personal journey. It is about finding the answer and your place under the sun, wherever that may be. The answer will be different for everyone because of our uniqueness in the world.

Yet, in spite of our unique nature, there are common elements that comprise the answer for all of us. Once you discover the answer, your life will change in a way that you never dreamed possible. Here is one answer that you can implement today. Make it a goal to eliminate your credit card debt. If you have several credit cards, reduce them to one card. You only need one credit card to make air and hotel reservations. When the bill comes in, pay it and avoid paying finance charges. Hippocrates once said, "Everything in excess is opposed to nature."

This book covers multiple areas in both your personal and professional life. The true secret to your success both at home and at work is to apply strategies that will impact the outcomes of your life. The strategies are based on sound, scientific principles as well as the wisdom of the ages. It blends the elements of science and philosophy into a cohesive, easy-to-understand strategy that you can apply daily. For example, most people today readily understand that the employment bond with their employers is at best tenuous.

Ever since the massive layoffs during the tumultuous 1980s, employment movement in and out of organizations is now commonplace. While some companies still enjoy loyal and tenured employees, the odds are against it long term. In fact, most people will have ten to fifteen or more jobs over the course of a lifetime. Many will have multiple careers as well. One of your goals is to figure out your best career without experimenting with careers. Your career is not a crapshoot. Your life should not be based on the dictates of others.

According to a recent survey by the Bureau of Labor Statistics, nearly fifteen million people are out of work. This includes both the short- and long-term unemployed. Hopefully, as the seventy-six million baby boomers in the United States slowly start to retire from the workforce, job openings will increase. Companies will eventually be competing fiercely for a shrinking pool of talent. While some may argue that the labor pool is not that sparse, the pool for skilled labor is. Anyone can flip burgers, but you need skills to fix a diesel engine or manage a department.

What can you do to manage your career in a job-churning work environment? It does not matter if the ride lasts for five or twenty years; what does matter is the quality of the engagement while you are on the payroll. Is there a strategy for a well-planned career? I believe there is. Having a well-planned career strategy will help prepare you for your next opportunity or promotion. At the same time, your company will reap the benefits of a person on a mission to excel. There is an excellent chance that your current employer will not be your employer within the next three to five years. One benchmark we often hear is that it takes one month for every $20,000 of income to find a new job. If you're making $60,000, then it could take you three months to obtain new employment. However, in a down economy, it can take you much longer to secure a new job.

Who can afford to be out of work for three months, let alone two years? If you're living in abject poverty, who can afford to be out of work one day? The monthly bills keep on coming, and not everyone will have the luxury of a severance package. The time to start getting a job in ninety days or less is now. What I can offer you here is a three-month program to get your career on track. Don't delay! What happens if you suddenly find yourself on the unemployment line? You will be ahead of the game if you adopt the strategies discussed in this book.

Key Points

1. There is a strategy for securing a new job in ninety days or less. The key is to follow the strategies outlined in this book.

2. The well-spent life is not an accident. It requires diligence, perseverance, and a desire to pursue your passions and purpose in life.

3. The worst-case scenario is to be at death's door and suddenly realize you did not fulfill your goals or purpose in life.

4. From the moment of conception, you came into this world for a reason.

5. Avoid spending a lifetime that is totally out of alignment with your passion, preferences, and true purpose in life.

6. You are the chief architect of your economic destiny. Pay off your debt and limit your use of credit cards.

7. There is a strategy for a well-planned career.

8. This book provides you with a ninety-day strategy to get a great job. Reading about it is one thing. Implementing the action steps is where the real work begins.

One

FIND YOUR PASSION: GETTING THE GOLD REQUIRES A LITTLE DIGGING

"Nothing great in the world has ever been accomplished without passion."

- Christian Friedrich Hebbel

There is a lot of discussion these days about the importance of understanding your life's purpose. I have made the case that your inner voice has a lot to do with your purpose in life. Whether or not that is important is for you to decide. However, if you are serious about getting your career on track in ninety days or less, you must determine your purpose or mission in life. Your job is more than a resume and a paycheck. It is, in most cases, a full-time commitment that should align with your purpose, passion, preferences, and goals. If you are not in alignment, you will not be as happy as you could be. It's that simple.

Many people have found employment without giving one second of thought to their life's purpose. They don't have a clue. All they know is that the bills need to get paid and they have to work. Just think about all those people who say, "Thank God it's Friday." There is a mismatch between their dreams and reality. A mismatch in your chosen field does nothing but waste time, energy, and fulfillment. There are people making six figures who drown themselves in martinis every night. There has got to be a better way to achieve happiness and fulfillment.

Your purpose or mission is directly linked to your inner voice. Your inner voice is that invisible force or cosmic energy that is located somewhere in the cobwebs of your mind. You can't see, smell, or touch it, but it's there. As long as you are alive, it is within you. When you die, it will abruptly depart. Cosmic energy cannot live in dead people. It serves no purpose. Your purpose will often surface as a gut instinct, hunch, or even in a dream when you wake up in the middle of the night startled by a revelation. Sometimes you will be daydreaming, driving, or taking a shower when suddenly your inner voice starts communicating with you. Instead of rolling over and going back to sleep, you should get in the habit of writing those thoughts down while they are still fresh in your mind. This notion of your inner voice or the soul is supported by many great philosophers in history.

"Pure practical reason postulates the immortality of the soul, for reason in the pure and practical sense aims at the perfect good *(summum bonum)*, and this perfect good is only possible on the supposition of the soul's immortality. It is the moral law which determines the will, and in his will the perfect harmony of the mind with the moral law is the supreme condition of the *summum bonum*."

- Immanuel Kant, The Immortality of the Soul

Summum bonum is a Latin term meaning the greatest or supreme good in which all moral values are included or from which they are derived. Your invisible self, therefore, has good intentions. There is a big difference between "life purpose" and "passion." If you Google "life purpose," you will yield over eighty-four million hits on the Internet! You will see things like "Seven Simple Questions to Help You Determine Your Life Purpose," "Discovering Your Life Purpose," and "What's My Life Purpose?" You can even attend life purpose seminars or hire a life purpose coach who can help you figure out the reason why you are here on earth.

All of these life purpose gurus can play a very positive role in your life. However, I'm here to tell you that trying to figure out why you are here on earth is a very difficult endeavor. Clearly, it is not an easy task to figure out your true purpose. It is a mystery. Your inner voice does not have a tongue. It cannot speak and literally tell you what to do. Perhaps we were meant to embark on a self-discovery process. Who knows? In fact, it is almost impossible for you to even relate to your sub-conscious mind. If that were not the case, chances are you would have figured out your purpose by puberty.

This is a book about you getting a job in ninety days. So why not leave the inner voice thing out of the picture? I can't do that. I am firmly convinced that if you are going to reach your full potential in life, you have to bring in the inner voice. You have to discover your passion and your purpose. Can you succeed in life without going through this process? Of course you can. But you may never achieve your full potential.

And when you die, you will no doubt sense, "I missed the mark."

Many life purpose gurus will tell you that you have a very definite mission on earth. Some believe you may return to the earth multiple times after death. A fundamental belief for people practicing Hinduism and Buddhism is reincarnation, which means that upon death, you come back to earth in another body or form. If you accept the logic that earth is a training school, then it would make sense for you to come back in the event you failed to graduate during your previous life.

General George Patton believed in reincarnation and thought he was, in a previous life, Carthaginian General Hannibal. The goal for people who believe in reincarnation is to aim for perfection. You keep coming back, possibly once every fifteen hundred years until you get it right.

To my knowledge, there is no evidence of the concept of reincarnation. Yet no one really knows the true answers to all the mysteries in the universe. Is there such a thing as reincarnation? I'll let you know in the next life.

Your purpose in life may unfold as you live your life. Trying to figure out your life purpose right now is a very difficult endeavor. For me, life purpose and understanding the objectives of your inner voice are one and the same. It may be more practical to figure out your life's purpose by concentrating on your passions. Your passion will be your best barometer to move you in the right direction and to bring you a sense of fulfillment. Your passion will help you connect with your inner voice. It's also a lot easier to figure out.

According to the *Random House Dictionary of the English Language*, "passion" is defined as any powerful or compelling emotion or feeling. It has other meanings, too, of course, such as love, sexual desire, and anger. When we were kids, we were filled with passion. We had nothing to hide. If your brother took one of your toys, you probably went crying to Mommy. When we laughed, we often fell on the floor, completely out of control. As we grew older, we learned things like manners, etiquette, and proper behavior, and for some of us, our emotions slowly began to recede into the hidden corners of our mind. Most kids are totally uninhibited.

Robert Louis Stevenson once said, "For God's sake give me the young man who has brains enough to make a fool of himself." Kids often say and do things without ever thinking it might get them into trouble. I remember one day in elementary school, on Valentine's Day, we were permitted to write notes to classmates. So I wrote an innocent little note to one of my friends and signed it "Mr. X." After the teacher read the note aloud in class, she became furious and demanded to know who wrote it. She was apparently not amused by my signature. I was laughing so hard, I gave myself away and was promptly escorted to the principal's office.

Here's the point: You need to get rid of your emotional straitjacket. You need to go back in time and recapture the things that really made you happy and excited when you were a kid. Rekindling those passions will help to determine if you are on the right career track in life. It's important to find your passion, because you will live a happier and more fulfilling life. Now how do I know that? I have been personally pursuing my passions for years. When I am writing, hours can literally slip by into the early hours of the morning. When I'm speaking before a large audience, my passions are in full thrust. The last thing you want is to work at some job for twenty years and realize you hate what you're doing. And, by the way, it's never too late to start this process. If you're approaching retirement, just think of all of those years you can devote to your newly found passion.

Passion is not looked upon fondly by many philosophers—especially those who lived in the nineteenth century. Many of these philosophers reduced passion to a lack of reason or self-control. More often than not, they were thinking of lust. The passion that I'm talking about is the source for your enthusiasm for something that is close and dear to your heart. John Maxwell once said, "A great leader's courage to fulfill his vision comes from passion, not position."

So what is this thing called passion? Well, it's complicated. People are complicated. There are no easy answers. Passion is the steam that propels us forward, yet there are negative and positive passions. Let me begin by telling you what negative passion is. If you hate getting out of bed in the morning to go to work, you're suffering from negative passion. If you hate your boss (by the way, the majority of resignations have to do with a poor working relationship with the boss), your passion is in the toilet. If you can't wait for the clock to strike 5:00 p.m. (quitting time), you probably loathe your job. By the way, most surveys indicate that approximately 60 percent of people are not engaged in their work. Why? They are miserable. If you hate the house you live in and feel depressed as you approach the driveway, that's a severe case of negative passion. There's nothing worse than going from a miserable job to a miserable house. Not really. There are worse things in life. Some people live on a park bench or wait for the local soup kitchen to open to get some food in their belly. Are you beginning to see the picture? Positive passion lifts you up. You feel invigorated. You have a sense that you can conquer the world and nothing can stop you.

The problem with passion is that reality and practicality kicks in. You may have to pay rent or a mortgage. Perhaps there's a monthly car note. Let's not forget about the utility bills. Your credit card debt is creeping upwards. The kids need to go to college. You may be well paid in your job and feel comfortable. You might have a corner office, executive status, and a six-figure income. Perhaps you have been with the company for ten or more years, and you've made some friends. You have developed habits and routines and don't want to change. Change can be difficult. You don't want to leave because even though you hate your job, life is good. You feel comfortable in your surroundings. You enjoy doing lunch with your colleagues. So you dig in, put your head to the grindstone, and plow forward. When the boss comes in, you do your best to make him or her happy. Then you develop a knot in your stomach and blame it on last night's dinner. I'm not sure if I would call this a life. It might be referred to as an existence. Before you know it, you're having two merlots a night and falling asleep on the couch with a potato chip between your fingers. This may be a sorry, pathetic picture, but I'm sure you can think of worse situations with people you know.

Finding your passion can absolutely be a new lease on life. It does not have to be a traumatic change. I'm not asking you to quit your job tomorrow or leave your spouse to start chasing this newly discovered passion. Let's slow down a bit. The question that you need to work on right now is: How do you find your passion? How do you find that magic that will put a bounce in your step to help get that new job within ninety days? Where do you rediscover that passion that makes people think you're overdosing on super vitamins? You don't need to take any psychological or personality tests. You don't need to schedule an appointment with a psychologist. Look to your younger years for a few clues, and ask your friends and family for help. You simply need to ask yourself six very important questions and write down the answers.

1. What was or is your favorite pastime or hobby?

2. What did you want to be when you grew up?

3. What do your friends and family say you're really good at?

4. If you could do anything you wanted and money was not an issue, what would you do?

5. What are your dreams or fantasies that sometimes wake you up in the middle of the night?

6. What do you sometimes do that can take hours, and yet you don't even notice the passing of time?

Create a Passion Statement

I have listed only six questions above. Please put this book down right now and answer them. Take a week if you have to. Just don't start reading the next chapter until you answer the questions. You will be doing yourself a disservice if you don't answer the questions first. Each question may generate more than one answer. Once you think of your answers, cut out the fat, reduce each answer to three or four lines, and create your own passion statement. Your passion statement is like your personal elevator speech. It is a short, succinct way of summing up what you want to accomplish in life. It is a statement of who you are and what you want to do in life. We're not talking about goals. Goals will be the action step you will implement to achieve your passion statement. Before you make your passion statement solid, discuss it with your spouse or best friends. Get their input. Use them as a sounding board. After discussing it, you may want to make some changes.

Once you have finalized your passion statement, you should carry it around with you at all times and read it often. Keep a copy of it in your wallet or purse so you can see it when you open your wallet. You need to read it often, because if you don't you will forget it. Reading your passion statement often will help reinforce it. Your brain will start to think of ways to accomplish it even while you're sleeping! Research indicates that even during sleep, our brain is processing memories and solving problems.

Here is my own passion statement:

Joe Carroll is an international speaker and author of great books.

His life's mission is to help people realize their full potential.

Helping others is a big part of my mission in life. I have this idea that when I go before the supreme cosmic ruler, he is going to ask me one question: What did you do to serve me on earth? Is this my inner voice speaking to me? My goal is to have a good answer. Yet, I fully realize it is not my good works or deeds, but the grace of God that is the deciding factor. Ninety days is right around the corner. Don't take more than a week to figure out your passion. Your passion is music to your invisible mind! So let's get with the program.

Key Points

1. Trying to figure out your purpose in life or your objectives is very difficult. An easier approach is to figure out your passion. Your passion is the bridge to your purpose in life.

2. It is never too late in life to pursue your passions. The choice is yours.

3. You need to get rid of your emotional straitjacket.

4. Your passion will give you a sense that you can conquer the world and nothing can stop you.

5. Create your own passion statement.

Two

YOUR PREFERENCES WILL KEEP YOU ON THE RIGHT PATH

"A successful life is one that is lived through understanding and pursuing one's own path, not chasing after the dreams of others."

- Chin-Ning Chu

I've seen it all before. The well-meaning coach has you list your top ten or twenty values, and then you are asked to put them in priority order. Once they are in priority order, you select the top ten, and these are the values you need to align with your job and your life. Some coaches make it more difficult. Instead of choosing values from a list, you are asked to write down what is important to you and then reduce these paragraphs to your top ten values, using one word for each value. Now that you know your values, you are home free. I don't think so. This is not the real world. In addition, your values are not anywhere close to your purpose or passion. Furthermore, your values can be flawed due to the influence of family and upbringing. You may need to cultivate new values to improve yourself and to achieve your goals in life.

Values can and will change like the wind. You may think you have core values today. These are values that you cherish, live, and die for. Five years later and your values can be totally different. Most people will abandon their values if it's a matter of survival. The mission of the self is not to die over a set of values. It is to get the mission accomplished. To make matters more complex, people compromise their values all the time. It's called job security. Do you think for one minute you are going to tell your boss off because what he just said compromises one of your precious values? If your boss tells you to do something, what is the likelihood that you will say, "Boss, let me think about how your game plan will fit in with my core values." Of course, you can honor your values, tell your boss what you think, and then get fired. You can also shut up and deal with the stress of living a life that is not in alignment with your values. Finally, you can quietly seek other alternatives and eventually bring yourself closer to harmony. Is there another approach? Is there a better way to mesh your values with true happiness and success? I think there is.

First of all, there is far too much focus these days on "values" and how they are supposed to fit into your life's plan. Some coaches will say that values are at the core of your being and it is your values that determine what you will and will not do. I disagree. First of all, most people don't know what their values are, so how meaningful can values be in your everyday decision making? Secondly, your values are influenced by your family, friends, and the way you were raised. They are not necessarily your values. They are the values you grew up with. Thirdly, your so-called values, by influence, may in fact be the wrong values for you! Finally, when you are trying to figure out your values, you may come to the wrong conclusions. Having "courage" could possibly be a great value for you since it feels good to think you are courageous. But your inner voice, which is the architect of your passions, may have a whole different perspective about courage. Your inner voice may be telling you that you are not courageous. So, who are you going to listen to? Should you listen to your parents or your inner voice? Should you really rely on a list of twenty values that you picked from some list?

What exactly do we mean by the term "values?" There are all kinds of values relating to your personal life, work, family, society, and religion. According to Wikipedia.org, a value is a concept that describes the beliefs of an individual or culture. Another definition from en.wiktionary.org says that values are "a collection of guiding, usually positive principles; what one deems to be correct and desirable in life, especially regarding personal conduct."

So values are considered subjective and vary across people and cultures. Trying to mesh corporate values and personal values is almost an impossible task. Companies can try to get employees to live and breathe the values they are espousing, but in all actuality, a person's values may be in direct conflict with the corporate values. The only thing a company can do is to find a happy medium.

For me, values are not the connection between your passion and, ultimately, your life's purpose. I like to keep things really simple. My philosophy is not to try and figure out values. Instead, I would urge you to figure out your preferences. Preferences are something you can easily identify. A preference is basically your power to choose. Life offers you choices. Preferences are easier to determine than values. You can choose to work for a respectable Fortune 500 company or choose to work at a strip club. The choice is yours. At the end of the day, when you head hits the pillow at night, you need to think how you feel about working for that company or the strip club. You will either have a good feeling or a bad feeling. If your feeling is bad, than you probably made the wrong choice, and you will not be living up to your values, whatever they might be. For me, this is an easier road to travel.

Preferences are also easier to figure out. Do you prefer to work for a large company or a small company? Do you prefer to have one child or five children? Do you long for an advanced degree, or are you happy with a high school diploma? Do you prefer to work on diesel engines or teeth? Do you prefer to live in a warm climate or a cold climate? Do you prefer to make $50,000 or $100,000 or more for a living? Do you prefer to marry someone with blond, brown, red, or black hair? Do you prefer Asian, African, American, or Italian meals? The choice is yours. Don't get caught up in trying to figure out your values. When the time comes, your values will kick in and will help guide your actions. However, your preferences are a lot easier to figure out. It's less complicated. Once you figure out your preferences, then you can develop a game plan to achieve those preferences.

A preference, by definition, is a strong liking, a predisposition in favor of something, and offers you the right or chance to choose. Preferences are your inclinations, gut instincts, proclivities, and penchants. Your preferences are all about you and your likes and dislikes. Preferences fit very nicely in with my philosophy of life. Do you have a philosophy that you live by? If not, you should develop one. A philosophy will help you stay the course. It will keep things in perspective. It will enable you to make better decisions. Everyone under the sun should have a philosophy.

Here is mine:

Your passion, purpose, talent, and preferences need to be in alignment with your chosen profession.

Living a purposeful and compassionate life will lead to self-fulfillment.

What kind of country enables this type of philosophy to thrive? My America was founded, in part, on religious freedom and the belief in God. Fifty-six people pledged their support of the Declaration of Independence on July 4, 1776. Benjamin Franklin was seventy years old and the oldest signer. Two of the signers eventually became presidents: John Adams (second president) and Thomas Jefferson (third president). All of these men put their fortunes and their very lives at risk for an idea that they all believed in. They mention God in the very first paragraph. In the second paragraph they wrote the following:

"We hold these truths to be self-evident, that all men are created equal, that they are endowed by their Creator with certain unalienable rights, that among these are life, liberty, and the pursuit of happiness."

I don't know about you, but I get goose bumps whenever I read that passage. It is so inspiring. The founders included the term "Creator" in this document that forged the United States of America. My America is a country that believes in God. It is a country proud of its traditions. We are not an egalitarian society. However, we are a compassionate people and have programs and institutions to take care of the less fortunate. We are generous, caring, and give everyone the opportunity to succeed. But in the end, it will be your hard work in sync with your life's purpose that will enable you to fulfill your destiny.

Here is one very important thought about preferences. They should not simply center around you and your personal needs. Your one weakness with your preferences is that they usually are about you and not about the other guy or gal. Some of your preferences will hopefully benefit others as well. This is called compassion. According to Webster's dictionary, "compassion" means to have a sympathetic consciousness of others' distress together with a desire to alleviate it. Try to help a friend in need. This particular notion has withstood the test of time. It reminds me of an old story about the lion and the rat:

> One day a small rat surfaced from his nest to find himself between the paws of a huge sleeping lion, which immediately awoke and seized the rat. The rat pleaded with the fierce beast to be set free, and the lion, being very noble and wise, and in no need of such small prey, agreed to let the relieved rat go on his way.

Some days later in the same part of the forest, a hunter had laid a trap for the lion, and it duly caught him, so that the lion was trussed up in a strong net, helpless, with nothing to do than wait for the hunter to return.

But it was the rat who came along next, and seeing the lion in need of help, promptly set about biting and gnawing through the net, which soon began to unravel, setting the great lion free.

- Author Unknown

What goes around comes around. This magnificent universal law that has withstood the test of time comes down to one word—compassion. Of course, one moral to this story can suggest that even a lowly rodent can be of some use to animals higher up on the food chain. On the other hand, no good deed goes unnoticed. The lion let the rat live, and the rat repaid the favor.

The lesson to be learned here is: Don't dwell too much on your values. Instead, focus more on your preferences. They are easier to figure out. Once you figure out your preferences, you can develop goals and put an action plan in place to make your preferences become reality. It is also important to remember the Golden Rule. You were not placed on this earth simply to carry out your own personal objectives. We call this weakness selfishness. The person that helps others during their journey on earth is destined for glory—if not on earth, than certainly in heaven.

Key Points

1. Focus less on values and more on your preferences.

2. Preferences are easier to figure out.

3. Your life's purpose exists in the recesses of your mind. It drives your passions. Your passions drive your preferences.

4. Your preferences are no ticket to self-fulfillment. You must find room in your heart to be compassionate.

5. Preferences without goals are nothing more than pipe dreams.

6. Helping others and remembering the Golden Rule is your ticket to self-fulfillment.

7. A life without compassion is a life not worth living.

8. Your ultimate goal is self-fulfillment.

Three

YOUR TALENT IS THE KEY TO UNLOCKING YOUR DESTINY

"I believe that life is a journey, often difficult and sometimes incredibly cruel, but we are well equipped for it if only we tap into our talents and gifts and allow them to blossom."

- Les Brown

Now that you have worked out some of the details concerning your purpose and preferences in life, it's time to discover your talents. This is where your calling and your strategy come to a fork in the road. Later, we will talk about goals and action plans. Getting a job in ninety days or less also requires getting the right job based on your passion, purpose, and talents. To work in the wrong job and not use your talents is an absurd waste of time.

If you could predict your own future, what would you do differently to avoid this scenario? You love your job and have been working there for fifteen years. You're fifty years old, put in a sixty-hour workweek, and are well paid. You're called into your boss's office at eight o'clock in the morning. The human resources director is also there. Then you hear the bad news: I'm sorry, Jim; we had to make some cuts. You need to empty your desk. It was strictly a business decision.

This scenario is played out repeatedly in corporate America. We have been through eleven recessions. The 2007/2009 Great Recession is clearly the worst economy since the Great Depression in 1929. In this recession, there were six applicants for every job, according to the *New York Times*. At one point, approximately one out of every five males between the ages of twenty-five and fifty-four were unemployed. You need a strategy before a financial crisis hits home. But it's not just about the paycheck. It's not just about the job. It's about combining your passion with your talents into a cohesive strategy.

Having a strategy is like jumping out of a plane with a golden parachute. There are some risks. The ride is thrilling. The descent takes your breath away, and you land without breaking your legs. It's a wonderful strategy that will help make your career recession-proof. It's not about the twenty-year ride with the gold watch. In fact, if you stay with a company for twenty years, you're at a competitive disadvantage. We need change. Tires wear out. Air filters need replacing. When should you consider leaving a job? I recommend applying the career acid test. Ask yourself one question: Did the value of your accomplishments exceed your W2 earnings last year? You are an investment, and owners are looking for a return on their investment. This may sound cold and calculating, but that's life in the big city. We live in a capitalistic and entrepreneurial society. We are the envy of the world. My position is clear: the person who combines passion and talent will be an employer's most valuable employee.

When you are maximizing your talents, job security almost becomes a nonissue. Let me stress the word "almost." Life is filled with uncertainty and events beyond your control. However, it's important to understand that job security is dead in the water. You cannot rely on your company or the government to take care of you. You are responsible for your own economic destiny. If you fail to have a strategy, you're courting economic suicide. There will always be events totally out of your control. Therefore, even if you are in total alignment with your passion, talent, and strategy, you still need to manage your career.

Career management means managing your career moves. Gerald Abrahams tells us that "good positions don't win games. Good moves do." We need to accept the view that most of us will not remain with one company for life. Once you accept this view, then it makes sense to have an exit strategy. If we accept the view that many of us will have five to ten or more employers over the course of a lifetime, then it makes sense to have an exit strategy. It does not mean that you're disloyal or you hate your company. It simply reflects the reality of corporate life today.

Corporate life is too often locked into archaic job descriptions, inflexible time schedules, and flat training programs with little or no regard for talent, skills, needs, and the passions of today's remarkable workforce. It is very difficult, if not impossible, to apply your passions, preferences, and talents in an organization if you are in the wrong position. When your talents, passions, and preferences are in alignment with what you do for a living, that's when dreams turn into reality. It is a recipe for a no-regrets life.

There is no other society in the world that can match ours in terms of freedom, opportunity, and achievement. We have our collective talents to thank for our incredible progress! For goodness' sakes, we have landed men on the moon and returned them safely back to earth. We discovered water on the moon and Mars. We invented the artificial retina, enabling people blind for decades to see. We developed the artificial heart, turned water into fuel, invented the polio vaccine and the Model T Ford, sequenced the entire genome of a cancer patient, and created supercomputers that can now perform more than a quadrillion operations per second. So if you are an investment, and you need to perform well on the job, you really need to like your job. You need to have a strong preference for your job!

Many people just fall into jobs and that's why they fall short on jobs. Others go to college and major in law, chemistry, nursing, etc., because they think these fields are areas that they will enjoy or will be financially rewarding. Sometime parents push their kids into a particular field that the kids have absolutely no interest in. The average cost for a four-year college education is roughly $30,000. If you go to law school, your costs could easily climb to $175,000 or more, depending on the college you attend. Can you imagine spending this kind of money on an education and later determining that you want to do something else? Some mistakes are costly. You need to do your homework, especially if it's your parents who are footing the bill. Better yet, if you're planning on attending college, figure out how to pay for it yourself! I put myself through college after serving in the navy and taking advantage of the GI Bill. It didn't cost my mother a dime.

You need to align your passion and talent with your work. Ideally, this should be done before going off to college, but it's never too late to conduct a job alignment. Your passion statement will help you figure out what you should be doing for a living. You did create your passion before reading this chapter, right? If not, put this book down now and get to work on your passion statement!

You need to take the time to figure it out. Harland Sanders was the founder of Kentucky Fried Chicken, or KFC. He went through five careers before he finally figured out what he wanted to do. He was a fireman, insurance salesman, steamboat operator, tire salesman, and gas station operator. He was sixty-six years old, broke, and collecting a $105 monthly Social Security check when he started to travel throughout the United States to sell his chicken recipe. He lived out of his car because he could not afford to pay for a hotel room. Just going to the bathroom and taking a shower was a major challenge for this man. He knocked on 1,009 doors before he finally got a yes for his chicken recipe. The more noes you get, the closer you get to yes. Today, there are over eleven thousand KFC restaurants and Harland's picture is on every one of them. Imagine if he had started KFC at the age of thirty. Here's the point: Harland Sanders found his passion. He figured it out.

It's also important to factor in personality with your passions. Personality is the visible aspect of one's character as it impresses others (Random House). It's how we want the world to see us. However, what you show on the outside is not necessarily who you are on the inside. Personality is not necessarily a good indicator of who you are and what you should do. You should be aware of how others perceive you. It may give you a clue as to whether or not your passions are in full steam. While you're trying to figure it out, be wary of personality tests. Approximately, 36 percent of corporations use personality tests. Taking a personality test can be helpful. They're fun, interesting, and informative. They can help put you in the right direction, but not necessarily on the right road. They will tell you what you can do, not what you will do. There's a big difference between "can" and "will." It's called motivation. Edwin Chapman once said, "Whatever touches the nerves of motive, whatever shifts man's moral position, is mightier than steam or calories or lightning." You can bring a horse to a pond, but if that mare is not thirsty, there will be no ripples in that pond.

According to Myers Briggs, I would make a great police officer. I can assure you, my dream job is not becoming a member of the Miami Vice Squad! Tests only scratch the surface. Besides, how can you reduce 6.6 billion people down to four categories? It defies logic. We are too complex. Here is an easier approach. Ask your friends and co-workers to describe your personality. Knowing your personality will help you make the right career choices, especially if they are aligned with your passion statement.

Another important aspect of putting your passions to use is to recognize the talents you have. Talent is your natural ability. It drives your passions. It's a gift you were born with. It is not knowledge, skills, or interests. Knowledge and skills are developed. Interests can change. It is a myth that few people are talented. Everyone is born with unique gifts and talents. It's in your DNA. Discover your talents and use them on the job. Using your talents will help you achieve that no-regrets life.

How do you figure out your talents? Here are a few pointers:

1. Ask your friends and relatives what you are really good at.

2. Do you have a hobby that occupies a lot of your personal time?

3. Did anyone ever compliment your accomplishing a particular task?

4. What particular activity or work gives you a feeling of fun and excitement?

5. Did you ever work on a particular project and the hours just seemed to fly by?

The answers to these five questions will help you to determine your true talents. Test your answers with your close friends and relatives to help you validate your answers. Once you identify your true talents, you have an obligation to nurture and develop those talents to their full potential.

Ingrid Bergman, the Hollywood movie star in the 1940s, once said, "I've never sought success in order to get fame and money; it's the talent and the passion that count in success." She was right on the money! Knowing your talents is not good enough. We need to use our talents. According to a Gallup Poll, only 20 percent of employees feel that their strengths are at play. And the longer you stay with the company and advance, the less likely you will play to your strengths. Tenure and long-term company loyalty are not good things. People get stale, and fruit withers on the vine. Even CEOs get tired of running their own companies. If you're not using your talents, you're wasting your talents and your company's money. Understanding your talents is part of the strategy. Talent is like electricity. If you don't use it, the lights don't go on.

So now you have a good grasp of your passions and your talents. Take a look at your current or last job. Does your job tap into your passions and talents? If it doesn't, what do you do? For starters, if you're working, I don't suggest you quit your job tomorrow, especially during times of high unemployment. Try to find ways with your current company to make better use of your talents. Perhaps you can transfer to a different department or take on additional responsibilities that are more aligned with your passions.

If you are looking for a new job, it will be easier to find that job if it takes advantage of your true talents. In fact, potential employers will absolutely see the value in hiring you if they can make the connection between your talents and their job description.

My passion is writing and public speaking. I am also a seasoned headhunter. I am very talented in recruiting. It's a talent, but not my strongest passion. I also write articles for magazines. I am an author and do a lot of public speaking. So I am pursuing my passions even though my main source of income is not related to my passion statement. If your job does include a lot of the things in your passion statement, then you need to do things to accelerate those job activities and bring your natural talents to even higher levels. The point here is that, even if you have raw talents, you still need to strive to develop that talent. Clark Gable is a Hollywood movie legend, but he did not become a legend overnight. It took him several years to become Rhett Butler in *Gone With the Wind*.

Key Points

1. When should you leave your job? Apply the acid test. Does the value of your accomplishments exceed your W2 earnings?

2. It is never too late to conduct a job alignment.

3. Since you may have five to ten or more employers over the course of a lifetime, it makes sense to have an exit strategy.

4. Once you identify your talents, you have an obligation to nourish and develop your talents to their full potential.

5. When your talents, passions, and preferences are in alignment with your job, then that is a recipe for a no-regrets life.

6. Your need is to strive for alignment or risk becoming an average participant in the game of life.

7. There is no other society in the world that can match ours in terms of freedom, opportunity and achievement. Consider yourself lucky if you are fortunate enough to live in the United States.

8. Many people just fall into jobs, and that's why they fall short on jobs.

9. What you show on the outside is not necessarily who you are on the inside.

10. There's a big difference between "can" and "will." It's called motivation.

11. Talent is your natural ability. It has nothing to do with knowledge, skills, or interests. It is incredibly important for you to figure out your talents and seek jobs that will maximize your talents.

Four

FITNESS: YOUR CHOICE—IT TAKES A LEAN HORSE TO STAY IN THE RACE

"Take care of your body with steadfast fidelity. The soul must see through these eyes alone, and if they are dim, the whole world is clouded."

- Johann Goethe

I personally struggle with body weight. I have been through many weight-loss programs over the years. I have tried all kinds of diets. I have joined gyms. Nothing lasted long term. Did you ever try getting out of a contract with a fitness center? Good luck. Regardless of the program, the fat comes in like a lion and wimps out like a lamb. Discipline is an art I am still working on. Self-discipline is a quality few people consistently practice. As they say, the first three letters of diet are "die." A lot of people that join gyms do not get their money's worth and eventually let their membership expire. I look upon diets as something temporary, and that's why they typically don't work long term for most people.

What should not be a shocking fact is that one third of all Americans will die due to either obesity or lack of nutrition. One third! I will tell you right now that I hate to exercise, but I sure don't want to become a statistic! The bottom line is that if we didn't work out, we wouldn't have the Olympics or sports, but we sure would have a lot more heart attacks. According to a researcher in Sweden, people who are overweight from a young age are at a greater risk of dying prematurely. Exercise is really important. Where would baseball, football, hockey, skating, and boxing be if people did not work out? Of course, we're not all jocks.

Yet there are also many successful people who are or were overweight. We don't have to be in prime condition to get the job done. Many notable examples exist, including King Henry VIII, Sir Winston Churchill, and Pavarotti, to name a few. How old were they when they died? King Henry died at the age of fifty-six from gout and syphilis. Pavarotti died of pancreatic cancer at the age of seventy-one. Churchill died of a stroke at the age of ninety.

However, if you want a fighting chance to remain healthy long term, you do need to eat right and exercise. Good health will make you a more productive worker. It increases your odds of having a quality life when you're old. Slim people look younger and generally have more energy. However, exercise does not provide any guarantees. All it takes is one drunk driver or a bad gene to propel your soul to the Milky Way. My own father was struck and killed by a car at the age of forty-seven as he was crossing a street in Jamaica, New York. The same fate happened with Margaret Mitchell, author of *Gone With the Wind*, when she was crossing a street in Atlanta. You can identify your passion as discussed earlier and know exactly what your calling in life is all about, but if you are dragging three hundred pounds of weight on your bones, you may be on the road to self-destruction, all because of one too many cookies or custard pies.

The leading cause of death in the United States is heart disease, according to the Centers for Disease Control and Prevention. The life expectancy in the United States for males is seventy-five and for females is eighty. That's a lot better than 1940, when the average age was sixty for males and sixty-five for females. We have science to thank for adding another fifteen years to our lives.

Shown below are the major causes of death per year in the United States of America:

1. Heart disease   631,636
2. Cancer   559,888
3. Stroke   137,119
4. Accidents   121,599
5. Diabetes   72,449
6. Alzheimer's   72,432
7. Nephritis   45,344
8. Septicemia   34,234

Source: Centers for Disease Control and Prevention

If you look at the American human landscape, we are pretty fat. We eat far too much food, and we eat the wrong foods. We consume too much red meat. We pig out on junk food and fast food. The lunches they serve in most school cafeterias are no better. We don't eat enough vegetables and are more likely to drink a can of Coke instead of a bottle of water. We have a multimillion-dollar industry in this country that survives on fat people. The profits are weighty. There are all kinds of gyms, diets, fitness trainers, health clubs, and weight-loss programs, and all of them are designed to get you into shape. The problem is that their efforts are not working very well.

According to the Centers for Disease Control and Prevention, in the United States, 67 percent of Americans age twenty and over are either overweight or obese. The trends are not getting any better. There have been no statistically significant changes in obesity in the United States since 2003. According to the American Obesity Association, 127 million adults in the United States are overweight, sixty million are obese, and nine million are severely obese!

According to another survey by the Centers for Disease Control and Prevention, less than half of American adults get regular exercise. We now have reality shows on TV with obese people competing to see who can lose the most weight. We are fascinated by these programs and marvel at the winners, but nothing changes in America when it comes to weight control. We take it off and put it back on. Where is the discipline? Are we like ancient Rome on the verge of collapse?

I am not an expert on weight control or proper diet. I do know that most Americans eat way too much food. In Japan, very few people are obese. The reason is really simple; they eat smaller portions of food. Their serving bowls hold approximately one-half to one cup of food. These are portions that we would normally feed our kids. And a lot of Japanese folks get around on bikes instead of cars or mass transit. They exercise more. As a result, lots of Japanese people are thin.

No one can make you exercise or eat the right foods. A big part of the problem is a lot of people are lazy. If you have a choice between the TV and the treadmill, most Americans will opt for the TV, especially if there are sufficient quantities of beer and potato chips. It may not be practical to get to work on a bike. However, there are things you can do.

To combat laziness, I want you to join a gym. I know I said before that most people are gym dropouts. Therefore, do not sign any long-term contract. However, if you join a gym that has both male and female members, this can work in your favor. It is a fact, for example, that men will work out harder and faster if they think a woman is looking at them. I don't know if this same fact holds true for women. But, if you're a man, this can be a great motivator.

Here is another strategy that I have used, and I can assure you I no longer have a weight problem. It's all about routines, reminders, and sticking to your master plan for success and happiness. I transformed half of my garage into a low-cost gym. There is not a day that goes by that I am not reminded that I have to work out. If you don't own a home, you can use part of your apartment to accomplish the same goals. It does not have to cost you a lot of money. Besides, whatever money you spend, it's an investment in yourself, and that's money well spent.

In my gym, I have the following:

1. Dumbbells and barbells
2. Exercise mat
3. Sit-up bench
4. Power tubes
5. Treadmill

The next thing you can do is go to a bookstore and pick up an exercise book. Once you know what to do, you start doing it on a regular basis. Establishing a routine will be the key to your physical success. Pick a time either before work or after work, and stick to a schedule. Work out for a minimum of thirty minutes a day. If you can squeeze in sixty minutes, that's even better. Take Sunday off for good behavior. Remember, it does not take a lot of exercise to keep your body in shape, provided you are not overloading it with the wrong foods. However, you must break a sweat. If you are not sweating, then you did not exercise enough. I have to be on the treadmill for about an hour to break a sweat. With my workout on the treadmill, I lose about four hundred calories in one hour.

Count your calories. You need to know how many calories you consume on a daily basis to avoid putting on additional weight. You need to weigh yourself every day and measure your neck and waistline. Maintain a log. This counting does not have to be forever. You just need to get a sense of how much you are consuming and how much you need to cut back.

My diet is pretty Spartan, and it's usually less than two thousand calories a day. Here it is:

1. Breakfast: cup of tea or coffee and a whole wheat muffin. Sometimes I will only have a twelve-ounce energy drink or a bowl of bran cereal.

2. Lunch: either an orange or energy drink.

3. Midday: another energy drink.

4. Dinner: fish, chicken, or meat with a vegetable, and two oatmeal cookies. You're better off skipping the cookies.

5. Water: six to eight glasses per day.

6. Sleep: I try to get between seven and eight hours a night.

Generally, it's a good idea to eliminate or reduce your consumption of sugar, salt, and artificial additives. I know, easier said than done. Once you are aware that these things are not good for you, you will reduce your intake. Also be careful of your alcohol intake. Alcohol is a toxin and harmful to your body. Obviously, elimination of all alcohol is the best thing. If you must drink, I would limit it to wine, preferably red wine.

Do I ever cheat on the above routine? Of course! I'm human! If there is a party in the office, and there is cake, I might have a small slice. If I am doing lunch with a client, I might occasionally have dessert. Going off routine is encouraged so your mind does not think it is being horsewhipped into losing weight without any options for adventure. Humans were raised in the wild. We grew up with risk and adventure every day. It was a matter of survival in the early days. We need to keep some of that Stone Age attitude with us today. Our bodies and genetics have not changed as rapidly as our intellect. Sometimes we still need to pretend we're running away from the tiger.

Just remember, when we were in the wild, we did not consume granulated sugar, table salt, or alcohol. It was mostly vegetables, fruit, and water. Fish and meat came later, after we learned how to catch them. We may have the mind of modern man, but our bodies have not progressed as rapidly in the evolutionary sense of the word. Our bodies still think it's all about fruits and vegetables. If your liver and kidneys could talk, you know what they would be saying? "There he goes again! He's feeding me more junk food!"

The bottom line is this: Looking for a new job requires a lot of energy. You need to be in top shape to get the top job of your choice. Exercise also helps eliminates stress, which is often a by-product of unemployment. Stress is not something that will help you perform well during an interview. Let's eliminate the stress and tone up the body all at the same time. Remember, your body is the house your soul is currently residing in. Let's make your soul feel like it has first-class accommodations!

Key Points

1. Most diets are short-term solutions and do not get the job done long term.

2. One third of all Americans die because of obesity or lack of nutrition.

3. You have a choice regarding body maintenance. Eating right and exercising will increase your odds of having a quality life when you're old.

4. Exercise is all about routines, reminders, and sticking to your master plan for success and happiness.

5. Get your daily intake of calories below two thousand. Thin is in and fat is out.

6. Eliminate or reduce your consumption of sugar, table salt, artificial additives, and alcohol.

7. Life is unpredictable. It's OK to break your routines once a while.

8. Living a healthy lifestyle will make it easier for you to land that job in ninety days or less.

Five

TEN JOB SECRETS THEY NEVER TAUGHT YOU IN COLLEGE

"It is a thousand times better to have common sense without education than to have education without common sense"

- Robert Green Ingersoll

These secrets were developed through the school of hard knocks. This chapter is, no doubt, one of the best chapters in this book. Read it slowly. I am a big believer in learning from my own mistakes and gaining wisdom from smart people. My attitude is, why spend five years making the same stupid mistakes when you can learn from a master and get it down to a science? So take these secrets to heart and make these pointers part of your daily routine:

1. **Finding jobs means dialing for jobs.**

Most people engaged in job search activities rarely pick up the phone to find a job. They invariably rely on the Internet, job boards, job fairs, and other safe, low-risk, nonaggressive techniques in finding employment. While these activities can be helpful, the odds of your finding a job through the traditional approach is extremely low. Yet, there are job hunters who will literally sit in front of their computer for hours and transmit hundreds of their resumes to organizations who will not have the decency to respond back with a short acknowledgment. Welcome to the world of cyberspace, utter discouragement, and the eternal black hole. There is a better way.

Using the phone can be a powerful way of uncovering unpublished jobs. In fact, it is so important that I have devoted an entire chapter to this technique. You absolutely need to get over the fear of using the phone. Calling someone you may not know can be very difficult. This is why most people do not pursue a sales career. However, if you want to truly land your great new job in ninety days or less, you need to make the phone your best friend. I will help you to smile and dial. It's not as hard as you think it is. We'll talk more on this subject later.

2. **It's not what you know, it's who you know.**

Many organizations will actually hire someone they remotely know who may be less qualified rather than someone they don't know who is more qualified. Of course, this practically defies logic, but it is the real world. We simply prefer not to hire strangers. Ever since we were kids, our parents told us not to talk to strangers. Trust is a major factor in the employee/employer courtship, and a stranger does not inspire trust. Employers want to feel comfortable with a new employee. They want confidence that the new hire will be a good fit and will blend in with the culture of the organization. Nobody wants to make a poor hiring decision. How do employers find that comfort zone they are seeking?

Many employers hire new people through an internal referral process because it increases the comfort factor. In fact, some research suggests that employee referrals yield the highest quality of new hires for most employers. Many companies pay their employees a referral bonus for recommending new people. They figure that birds of a feather flock together. Companies also know that their employees will not recommend an undesirable candidate because it would be a negative reflection on them. Here is a very important point:

Career positioning requires that you get to know people in other organizations who will not hesitate in recommending you to people in their organizations.

You need to read the above quote one more time. It is really important.

If the company's recruiter has three hundred resumes, and your friend who works in the facilities department recommends you, your resume goes to the top of the list. Your networking activities will also benefit your company in many ways. Networking can lead to terrific new hires and may also result in new business for your company.

3. **Staying in your field increases your earning power.**

Many times when people suddenly find themselves unemployed, they start to consider other job options, such as starting their own business or going down the consulting route. This is often a very emotional decision, which, by the way, is not all that bad. Some, out of frustration or negative feelings about their last position, decide that they want to try something different. If you are in between jobs, there is no better time than now to source for a job that will be in alignment with your purpose, passion, and talents. Financially, you may have to pay a price for this happiness.

Companies are not going to hire you for your good looks, starched shirts, and three-button suits. They will hire you because of your skill sets. They want to know what value you bring to the table. How are you going to help lower costs and improve systems and processes? Employers know that past performance predicts future behavior. In your current field, you are a known quantity. Hiring managers can predict how well you will do based on past performance. If you're going into a new field, it's a risk. I'm not suggesting that you avoid risk. In fact, I encourage risk. Your gut instincts will tell you if you are up for the challenge. However, if you decide to change fields and try something different, you automatically increase the likelihood of taking a pay cut. It may cost you big-time from a financial perspective. Be sure you can handle a pay cut. However, long term, the decision can pay off. Are you willing to take a chance?

4. **Don't ignore the power of a name or reference.**

One of the classic blunders for the novice job hunter is to send resumes to a blind ad, a human resources department, or an e-mail address that does not identify the hiring manager. If you prefer to get your new job in ninety days or less, you need to target your audience. It is important to identify your next boss or someone who can recommend you to your next boss. Research becomes critical if you are to successfully identify specific names and job titles of individuals in your target company. There are various ways to uncover this information.

Try to think like a headhunter. How do you think headhunters uncover names of people in organizations? They research publications like the Book of Lists and sources such as Dun and Bradstreet or Hoovers. They find names in various associations and attend networking meetings. They go directly to company Web sites or cold-call companies. They network with people in organizations to find names of other people in those same organizations. It requires a little detective work. The bottom line is that you never want to go down a blind alley. Get the name and you will increase your odds of getting the job.

5. Never ask for a job, but always ask for a referral.

This sounds almost contrary to your main objective. You may be out of a job, and I'm advising you not to ask for a job? Am I nuts? I can assure you that I am not nuts. When you are networking with other people or scheduling meetings with potential employers, you need to diffuse the situation by taking the pressure off. If you ask someone for a job during your networking activities, chances are that he or she will not have a job to give you. The no-job-opening response will quickly end the conversation. People feel uncomfortable when they cannot help, and their instinct is to end the call as quickly as they can. Do not ask for a job.

Begin your conversation by taking a sincere interest in the person you are talking with. Look for ways you can help him or her. Instead of asking for a job, you are better off asking for a referral. Many people will be able to help you with their referrals because they know people that you don't know. It also enables them to help you. Most people want to help.

6. **Don't waste your time with recruiters unless they seek you out.**

I have nothing against recruiters. I was once a recruiter. Been there and done that. They can and do perform a valuable service and are quite good in connecting job seekers with employers. What some of us forget is that recruiters are working for the company, not you. They are paid by the employer. It is also a timing game. If they happen to be working on a placement and your background is a perfect match for their client, you may have a chance. If you send them your resume, it will be stored electronically and may never surface again on their radar screen. In fact, you will be lucky if they even bother to send you a letter acknowledging receipt of your resume. Don't take it personally. They don't have the time, motivation, or resources to respond to unsolicited resumes. Most recruiters find candidates based on very specific job criteria. The best advice I can give you is to try to be discovered by a recruiter. Mingle where they mingle. Join an organization where they hang out and volunteer for committee work. Getting your name out there can often result in a recruiter finding you.

7. Get the job before the company advertises it.

The 80/20 rule means that 20 percent of the people will achieve 80 percent of the results. Apply this concept to the job search context and you will discover that 20 percent of the people find jobs before they are advertised, while 80 percent of the job hunters are responding to ads in the newspaper and the Internet. The problem with responding to ads on job boards or in newspapers is competition. You instantly may have three hundred other people wanting and applying for the same job. This often results in your resume being glanced at for fifteen seconds and then winding up in the reject pile. If you want to beat out the competition, you need to uncover those job opportunities before they hit the mass media.

8. Know exactly what you're looking for.

It is amazing to me how many people start a job search and have no clue what they want to do. This is why it is so important to have your passion statement completed. The last thing a potential employer wants to hear about is uncertainty. You need to figure out exactly what you want to do and be able to communicate your career objectives in a very succinct way. Another problem is that many people try to use the shotgun approach. They figure if they throw enough skill sets on the wall, something might stick with a potential employer. Employers prefer the sharpshooter approach. The more specific and laser beamed you can be in terms of what you can do, the more valuable you become in the eyes of the hiring manager.

You also need to nail down your thirty-second elevator speech. What is it that you bring to the bargaining table, in a nutshell? Avoid talking about your magnificent triumphs. Instead, think like a salesperson and talk about the benefits you can bring to the table. For example, instead of saying, "I am a facilities manager with ten years of experience," say something like, "I help companies reduce their facilities management operating costs by an average of 30 percent." If you were the hiring manager, which line would you prefer to hear?

9. **You must follow a consistent and repeatable process.**

The people that find jobs sooner and not later have a search model and stick to it. Finding a job is a full-time job. It requires a consistent process that you apply daily. It's like exercise. If you stop working out, your muscles will start to soften up. You need to apply your model every day. In addition, networking should be a critical component in your job search. Try to develop a network of fifty people and nurture this network like family. Call your network on a periodic basis. Send birthday cards. Go to lunch and find ways to help them.

By maintaining a consistent and repeatable process, you will maintain a pipeline of potential opportunities. If your pipeline dries up, so will your job prospects. You always need to have a full pipeline. This requires a lot of persistence. You must have a willingness to work on the pipeline. It will definitely shorten your job search.

10. **Executives need to harness the power of humility.**

If you are a high-level executive and have suddenly found yourself in between jobs, try and put your ego in check. In fact, put your ego somewhere in the closet and don't let it out again until after you have your new job. I know, for some this may be easier said than done. You have been in the commander's seat and totally in control. You had people at your beck and call. You have developed this air of confidence and felt that nothing could stop you. You were held in high regard by your neighbors, co-workers, and colleagues. You felt invincible, solid, and very successful, and suddenly you are walking out the door with your severance package between your legs. Many executives are not savvy job hunters. They are not often in the situation where they are in between jobs. Most will rely heavily on one of the well-known, national executive recruiters. My word of caution is this: do not put all your eggs in one frying pan. They may all get burnt. You need options and alternatives.

You also need to get over the shock of job loss real quickly. It's almost like a member of the family dying. Most executives do not do well when they sense things are out of control. Many put on their poker face and leave the impression that this is a minor blip in their rise to success and fortune. My advice to you is to quickly get rid of the attitude, develop a sense of humility, and start to lean heavily on your network in a nice and friendly way. You are not the first executive to be let out on the mean streets. Your attitude, demeanor, and friendly smile will do more for you than any high-priced executive recruiter. Again, this is not to demean the usefulness of recruiters. They do a good job. You do need more options.

Key Points

1. Make the phone your best friend. It is the ticket to clinching job offers within ninety days or less.

2. Career positioning requires you get to know people in other organizations who will not hesitate to recommend you.

3. Staying in your field increases your earning power, but leaving it may accelerate your passions in life.

4. Try to think like a headhunter instead of a job seeker.

5. Your main focus is learning how to help others first.

6. The goal is to get the job before the company advertises the job.

7. The choice is simple: know what you want and follow a consistent and repeatable process to achieve it, or let the chips fall where they may.

8. High-priced executives need to check their egos at the door.

Six

MASTER THE PHILOSOPHY OF SELF-FULFILLMENT

"However beautiful the strategy, you should occasionally look at the results."

- Sir Winston Churchill

So far, we have talked about passion, preferences, and talents. We also talked about the need for getting in shape and learned about some gems in job search strategies. All of these great ideas and activities are meaningless unless we have a strategy or philosophy for living. The very worst thing that we can think of is the thought of dying and not getting a chance to fulfill our life's work or destiny. Yes, everyone has a destiny. The question is, how much control do we have over our own destiny? The astrology advocates will tell you that your life is already planned out and somehow connected with the moon and the stars.

Personally, I don't believe that destiny is predetermined. We were all born with free will. We make the earthly decisions and are held accountable for those decisions. Your destiny is not inevitable or unchangeable. We may not be able to change the laws of the universe, but we have absolute control over the laws of self to a degree. I have previously suggested that it will be easier for you to land a job and maximize success if you adopt the philosophy of self-fulfillment. Mastering this philosophy will help you along your journey to new employment. I repeat this philosophy again because, as Napoleon Hill once said, "Any idea, plan, or purpose may be placed in the mind through repetition of thought."

Your passion, purpose, talent, and preferences need to be in alignment with your chosen profession.

Living a purposeful and compassionate life will lead to self-fulfillment.

Can you get by in life without this philosophy? Of course you can. However, I believe everyone should have some guiding principles to help keep them on track and to steady the course. A philosophy of thinking can help in this endeavor tremendously.

We make choices and decisions every day for better or for worse. You are "the master of your fate and the captain of your soul." This famous line was immortalized in the poem "Invictus," written by the English poet William Ernest Henley. He wrote the poem when he was twenty-six in 1875. He was in a hospital in Edinburgh, where complications from tuberculosis necessitated the amputation of his leg. The man was an atheist until the day he died at the age of fifty-three. While it is said he did not believe in God and the afterlife, I find it interesting that he thanks "gods" and mentions his soul in one of the lines of his poem. Clearly, his poem resonates with the strength of the human spirit:

Out of the night that covers me,
Black as the pit from pole to pole,
I thank whatever gods may be,
For my unconquerable soul.

In the fell clutch of circumstance,
I have not winced nor cried aloud,
Under the bludgeonings of chance,
My head is bloody, but unbowed.

Beyond this place of wrath and tears
Looms but the Horror of the shade,
And yet the menace of the years
Finds and shall find me unafraid.

It matters not how strait the gate,
How charged with punishments the scroll,
I am the master of my fate,
I am the captain of my soul.

- William Ernest Henley, 1875

You determine your own destiny by the choices you make daily. Of course, your choices can be disrupted by the choices of other people. Poor timing, bad luck, and being in the wrong place at the wrong time can impact your life forever. In some cases, it can cause people to die at an early age.

Viktor Frankl is an example of how someone escaped the jaws of death. Frankl was one of Europe's top psychiatrists who developed a revolutionary approach to psychotherapy called logotheraphy. His premise was that we can acquire a meaningful life through work, people, experience, attitude, or doing a good deed. Frankl was a Holocaust survivor. He was an incoming prisoner on one of two lines in the Auschwitz concentration camp. He was on the left line, which was going to the gas chambers. The prisoners on the right line were spared. As the lines moved, he slipped out of the left line and moved into the right line and survived. His wife, parents, and other family members were not as fortunate. Frankl had a preference to live, took a risk, and changed lines. Was it his inner voice that guided his thinking? Was it his survival instincts at work?

We choose to lean on the positive side of life and hope for a long and healthy life. The laws of karma tell us that the finality of your life is determined by the quality of your living. We get out of life what we put into life. If you want a glass of water, you need to fill the glass up with water. It's easy to make excuses or say you had a tough childhood or grew up on the wrong side of the tracks. I grew up in a city housing project called Pomonok in Queens, New York. It may have been a poor neighborhood, but ask any kid who grew up there and chances are he or she will tell you it was a wonderful childhood experience. If we want to achieve fulfillment in the real game of life, we need to adopt a self-fulfillment philosophy. Adopting a self-fulfillment philosophy is a key strategy for long-term happiness.

This type of philosophy encourages us to get things done and to be in alignment. It prevents procrastination from seeping in. It factors in the possibility that life can end abruptly on the short end of the stick. It forces us to make the most out of the time that we do have. We tend to want to hurry up because we are running out of time. Some advise us to slow down and chill out. Time runs out real quickly, especially as we get older. The well-lived life is all about what you contribute to life. I'm not talking about charitable contributions. It's not about living, taking, and dying. It's about living, giving, and doing. The Golden Rule, which has withstood the test of time, teaches us to do to others what we would have them do to us. Most people, by nature, want to do the right thing. They enjoy helping others when they can. It gives them a good feeling inside. This is a natural instinct for most of us. Truly, at the end of your time, these are the things that will bring you joy and comfort—that while I was here on this earth, I did some good.

Is there any scientific evidence to prove that helping others actually helps you? I think there is. One of the core answers that you can take to the bank is this: with some deviant exceptions, we are genetically wired to help our brothers and sisters. The individual who breaks ranks with this fundamental truth will eventually wind up on the short end of the stick, one way or the other.

During the 1970s, Robert Trivers wrote an article called "The Evolution of Reciprocal Altruism." His model demonstrates that under certain conditions, selection and survival favor altruistic behavior in the long run. One look at history proves his theories are correct. All tyrants of the world never succeed in the long run. Here are just a few, during the twentieth century, who eventually became social outcasts: Hitler, Stalin, Mao, Lenin, Pol Pot, Idi Amin, Mussolini, Tito, and Saddam Hussein. So what does any of this have to do with preferences, choices, outcomes, career management, and lifelong success?

Altruistic behavior in the workplace favors the successful executive. The self-centered executive who thinks that cheating and deceiving others for one's own selfish interests is OK eventually becomes the social outcast and even a jail felon. Two cases in point are Ken Lay and Jeff Skilling, found guilty in the Enron fraud and conspiracy trial. Too many companies are all about micromanagement and control. They tell people what to do and expect compliance. Great managers know that the best way to achieve superior performance is to ask questions and let their direct reports figure out the solutions. This is what empowerment is truly all about.

Most of us are good people. We want to do the right thing. It is our social barometer. It is also important to have a sense of what your mission is in life. When you examine your life, family, and career, you need to realize what you want to accomplish in life. Why are you here? You have a purpose in life. It's been coded into your DNA. The challenge is to determine what that purpose is. You determine your purpose by creating a passion statement. When you focus on a self-fulfillment philosophy, it forces you to think about who you are and what you want to accomplish. I encourage people to think in terms of what happens if you're running out of time. What do you need to get done today? We need to have a sense of urgency about life. Time is precious and waits for no one. Don't wait forty or fifty years to figure out your calling. However, even if you're sixty or seventy years old or older, it is never too late to figure out why you are here and what you need to do to fulfill your life's purpose.

Compassion is a major element in the self-fulfillment philosophy. It is a willingness to share someone's pain and to help them. It is the Golden Rule that has survived over the ages. In 500 BC in the *Analects of Confucius*, it is written: "What you do not want done to yourself, do not do to others." People get fired all the time because they do not practice the Golden Rule. If you were the owner of a company, would you want any of your employees demonstrating the following?

1. Spends too much time on personal activities instead of job activities.

2. Not respected by other members of the team.

3. Can't seem to get the job done in a timely manner.

4. Produces poor quality work.

Most of the above "termination triggers" can be avoided if you stop to think about the impact your shoddy work habits are having on team members or the company's performance. For example, would the quality of your work change if you knew in advance that your proposal would cause your company to lose the deal? If you're a hot-shot executive accustomed to talking down to people in a condescending way, would you think twice if you knew that productivity was suffering because of your arrogant rants? Think about your own behavior on the job and determine if you would fire yourself. If you went to unemployment to file a claim, do you think you would win the appeal if unemployment was denied?

When you develop a sense of compassion for others, it will often change your actions, habits, and how you interact with others. You will come across as more positive and helpful, and people will enjoy being with you. You will earn more respect and, in the eyes of your employer, you will increase your value to the organization. If there is a downsizing or perhaps a merger, you may be one of the survivors in the ensuing bloodbath.

Leo Durocher once said, "Nice guys finish last." With all due respect for Mr. Durocher, he absolutely has got it backwards. According to a study by Harvard University involving one hundred Boston-area college students playing the same game repeatedly, those that used punishment were the losers. Nice guys and gals do finish first in the game of life. It will be difficult for some people to develop altruistic behaviors. Perhaps you're not wired to wrap your helping hands around other people. You can change. You must change. The quality of your life depends on it.

Key Points

1. You make the choices in life and will be held accountable for those choices.

2. We get out of life what we put into life.

3. Can you say to yourself that while you were here, you did some good?

4. Altruistic behavior favors the successful executive.

5. When you focus on a self-fulfillment philosophy, it forces you to align your purpose and passions with what you need to be doing for a living.

6. Time is precious and waits for no one.

Seven

THE EIGHT THINGS YOU NEED TO KNOW ABOUT MANAGING YOUR CAREER

"Organization is not an option; it is a fundamental survival skill and distinct competitive advantage."

- Pam N. Woods

What do a messy office, credit card debt, and your neighbor's dog pooping on your front lawn all have in common? These are all examples of things we tolerate. Tolerations come in all sizes, both big and small. They can simply aggravate the living hell out of us. Tolerations tend to nag us daily. They cause us to lose focus on the important things in life. They rob us of our mental energy. They distract us and cause headaches and ulcers. The question is this: What can you do about them? The answer is actually quite simple.

Your goal is to either eliminate or fix the tolerations you are currently putting up with. Therefore, the first thing you need to know about career management is to fix your tolerations. This is important. If you are to conduct a successful job search within ninety days, you don't need a bunch of tolerations getting in the way of your objective.

Fixing your tolerations is like giving your mind a tune-up. It will make you feel free. It will give you added energy. It will make you feel like you now have time to conquer the world. It will help you focus on your career without getting bogged down in the minutia. We'll talk more about tolerations later in this book.

The second answer to career management is to figure it out. Don't wait until you're sixty or seventy to figure out what you want to do in life. But, even at that age, it is never too late. It gets back to the passion statement we talked about earlier. Your goal is to see the big picture. Start at the end of your life and reflect on what you would like it to look like. Then start making it happen.

The third answer to career management is to use your talents. Knowing your talents is not good enough. We need to use our talents. Kathe Kollwitz once said, "I do not want to die…until I have faithfully made the most of my talent and cultivated the seed that was placed in me until the last small twig has grown."

Activating your talent is critical. According to a Gallop Poll, only 20 percent of employees feel that their strengths are at play, and the longer they stay with the company and advance, the less likely they will play to their strengths.

The fourth answer to career management is to get excited or move on. If you are not excited about your job, the likelihood of your living up to your full potential is severely limited. Ask yourself if the following points describe your situation at work:

1. You can't wait to get to work.
2. Staying late is not an issue.
3. You're making a difference and others notice.
4. You are tapping into your talent and passions.
5. You are at the top of your game.
6. You feel engaged.
7. You are passionate about your work.

If you are not experiencing the above, then it's time to take a hard look at the choices you are making in life. Thomas Friedman, who wrote the book *The World Is Flat*, tells us we need to rediscover our inner fire truck. He would rather hire someone with a passion to learn and curiosity over a less passionate person who has a high IQ. Many of us are confronted with the choice of money versus happiness regarding the type of work we do. The answer is to make your career decisions based on what will make you happy. If you're not happy in your life's work, all the money in the world will not be enough to sustain your enthusiasm and success.

There was an interesting article in the *Wall Street Journal* concerning the actor Brian Dennehy, who appeared in some great movies like *Cocoon*. In the article, he says "I remember my father saying to me, 'What are you doing driving a cab and going to your stupid auditions?' And I said, 'I want to be an actor.' And he said, 'Why the hell would you want to be an actor?' 'Because I think it would make me happy.' " "What the hell has that got to do with anything?" was the disgusted response from Dad, a reporter for the Associated Press. Sometimes taking mom's and dad's advice is not always the best advice.

We often associate a fun job with waking up in the morning without an alarm clock. When we think of alarm clocks, the image of getting up for work in the morning immediately comes to mind. The problem with a lot of people and work is not the alarm clock, and it's not the job. Sure, a lot of people hate their job. What makes someone love his or her job while someone else hates theirs? It basically comes down to your thought patterns and what you do to overcome negativity.

Let's talk a bit about losing and finding a job. Millions of people have lost their jobs over the last few years. Perhaps you're one of them. If you have a burning desire to find a job within ninety days, you have to do more than just sharpen your focus on the job market. You have to go into survival mode and warp speed. How quickly it will take you to find a new job depends on how quickly you can get motivated and develop a winning attitude. Going through the motions of finding a job, making the right contacts, and showing up on time are all important aspects of the job hunt. However, if you don't like the job that you're trying to get, my advice to you, good friend, is to figure out what you really want to do.

There is a great book, available in most bookstores, called *What Color Is Your Parachute* by Richard Bolles. This book can really help you figure out what you like best without spending a fortune. Probably the biggest service our schools can provide our kids is to help them figure out what they should do in life. Every kid in high school should be required to take a course to help him or her determine what type of work he or she is best suited for.

Why waste years working in occupations that will eventually lead you to failure? A whole industry was created to help people who lost their jobs find new jobs. It's called outplacement. Most of these companies are paid very handsome fees by the company that just axed you. Why work for a company for ten years, get terminated, go to outplacement, and figure out you should have been doing something else? Don't waste time. It's over before you know it.

Whatever you do, don't spend years in a job that will require an alarm clock. You have unique talents and abilities. Put them to good use. Don't waste a lifetime chasing dollars. Give some thought about your chosen profession. Make sure you work for a just company that puts people and ethics at the top.

The fifth answer is to help others. Bruce Lee, the famous martial artist, once said, "If I should die tomorrow, I will have no regrets. I did what I wanted to do. You can't expect more from life." Helping others will help you to achieve a no-regrets life. When you mix tin, which is a soft metal, with copper, another soft metal, you get bronze, which is a hard metal. This is what we call synergy. When you help others, they help you to become stronger, wiser, and closer to living that no-regrets life that Bruce Lee worked so hard to achieve before dying at the young age of thirty-two.

The sixth answer is to know your score card. Babe Ruth was a pitcher. One day, early in his career, he made a career decision at the suggestion of a fellow teammate to stop pitching and focus on batting. He was a good pitcher. However, he was a great batter. The great Bambino hit sixty home runs in 1927 and kept that record for thirty-four years. He knew his talent and he kept his score. Do you know your talents and do you know your score at work?

The seventh answer is to write down your goals. John Goddard was the real Indiana Jones. He once said, "You need a plan for everything, whether it's building a cathedral or a chicken coop. Without a plan, you'll postpone living until you're dead." John Goddard was an amazing individual. At the age of fifteen, he wrote down 127 goals. Over the course of his life, he never stopped writing goals and has accomplished the majority of them. He followed Marco Polo's route through all the Middle East, Asia, and China. He explored the Nile River. That was his number one goal. He visited 122 countries, lived with 260 different tribal groups, and explored the Great Barrier Reef in Australia.

One way of looking at goals is to think of your own epitaph. An epitaph is a brief writing in praise of a deceased person. Pretend that you are deceased and recite your epitaph. Now why should I ask you to do something as morbid as writing your own epitaph?

The problem with most people is that they don't know what they want to accomplish in life. They don't realize how quickly life flies by. Don't wait until you're old and gray to accomplish your goals. To achieve your goals, you need to know your goals in advance. The best way to achieve your career goals is to start with the end product. Assume that you are well into your seventies. Don't sweat about not getting to that ripe old age. If you're a woman in the United States, you have a good shot at reaching eighty, and if you're a man, it's seventy-five. If you look at the entire planet of approximately 6.5 billion people, only about twenty-five actually reach the ripe old age of 110. Doesn't that make you feel good? Let's face it: life at 110 can be a little rough.

Let's move forward. Take some time to figure out exactly what you want the world to remember about you after you're dead and gone. Once your subconscious mind fully understands exactly what you want to do with your life, it will start helping you to achieve your goals. After you write your epitaph, record it on a tape recorder and then listen to it once in a while. It will help you to anchor it in your mind.

Every now and then, make it your business to update your epitaph. Progress does not stand still for people pursuing their dreams. When you record your epitaph, say it with feeling. After all, you are trying to convince your subconscious mind that these are the things that you truly want. When you play it back, play it loudly and don't miss a word. Remember, to reach your goals, you need to know your goals in advance.

Dr. Denis Waitley once said, "Most successful people believe in their own worth, even when they have nothing but a dream to hold on to." These next remarks are primarily for people just starting out. If your dream is to become an executive, have someone take a picture of you dressed like an executive, sitting behind a beautiful mahogany desk with a bookcase in the background. If you don't have such a desk, find a picture of someone in a magazine that portrays your goal image. Cut it out; replace the face in the picture with yours. Frame it and hang it on the wall and look at it at least once a day.

If your dream is to be a doctor, start looking like a doctor. Get your picture taken in a hospital emergency room with you fully equipped with the surgeon's cap, white coat, and stethoscope. If you want to be an engineer, put on a hard hat, go to a construction site, and have your picture taken looking at some blueprints.

Whatever your goal is, my friend, make it look real. Get a picture of it, blow it up, frame it, and place it over your bed so you see it every day of your life. As they say, a picture is worth a thousand words. Ivan Turgeniev once said, "A picture may instantly present what a book could set forth only in a hundred pages." If you make it easy for your mind to picture it, it will be easier for you to accomplish it.

The eighth answer is to find a hero. Sam Walton is my favorite hero. His success tips included:

1. Love your work.
2. Nose around for good talent.
3. Empower your employees.
4. Set high expectations.

5. Keep score.
6. Use well-chosen words of praise.
7. Have fun.

Sam Walton was the founder of a retail store. Today, the company is known as Walmart, the world's number one retailer with 6,400 stores, 1.8 million employees, operations in fourteen countries, and $315 billion in sales. If Sam were alive today, he would be the richest man in the world. Yet, all of Sam Walton's money could not save him from the ravages of cancer. He died in 1992 at the age of seventy-eight. Yet, he followed his passion and loved life. Flying planes and motivating his employees with pep talks kept him feeling young, vibrant, and excited about life.

Key Points

1. Conducting a successful job search requires eliminating your tolerations.

2. Write your own epitaph. Start at the end of your life and reflect on what you will like it to look like.

3. Activate your talent.

4. Get excited or move on.

5. Don't spend years in a job that will require an alarm clock.

6. By helping others, you help yourself.

7. Know your score card and write down your goals.

8. Fine a hero. We all need people to help inspire us.

Eight

GETTING FIRED CAN BE A BLESSING IN DISGUISE

"Fall seven times, stand up eight."

- Japanese Proverb

We have covered quite a bit of ground regarding your strategy for landing your job in ninety days or less. We have discussed passion, preferences, talents, exercise, self-fulfillment philosophy, and eliminating tolerations. This chapter focuses on the techniques you need to put into play to avoid the negative aspects of being unemployed. This chapter is one of the most important chapters in this book. Everything in life is based on perspective and your view of the future. Your view can be an asset or a liability, depending on how you think.

In 1931, two years after the Great Depression, eight million people were out of work. That was 25 percent of the workforce. The likelihood of another depression hitting the world economy is doubtful, but there will always be peaks and valleys on Wall Street. Job loss can be sudden and without warning. There is no such thing as job security. Donald Trump brought this reality close to him in his *Apprentice* show on television. Getting fired can happen to anyone at any time. How do you deal with it?

Steve Jobs was adopted at birth. He became the co-founder of Apple computers at the age of twenty-one in 1976. Nine years later he was fired. Eleven years later he became Apple's chief executive officer.

Larry King was fired at the age of forty from his radio show in Miami. He was in debt and off the air for three years. In 1978, at the age of forty-five, the *Larry King Live* show went national. It was the first nationwide call in show in history.

Lee Iacocca was fifty-four when Henry Ford fired him as president of Ford Motor Company. He later became president of Chrysler Corporation. Iacocca introduced the popular K car, repaid all of Chrysler's loans within five years, and turned the company around.

I provide you with these stories to encourage you. Some people give up hope and allow their dreams to fall off a cliff. You can take a different road. Do not fall into the trap of feeling sorry for your bad luck. Your attitude should be that you were lucky to get fired. Getting fired is not the end of the world. It is the beginning of a new and exciting journey. It does help to have a good sense of humor and a lot of self-motivation. You must remain positive internally and externally. When people see and talk with you, they should feel happy that they had the pleasure of spending some time with you. Your job, in part, is to leave everyone you talk to in a good mood. This strategy will help to put you in a good mood.

Lawrence Sterne, English clergyman and humorist, once said, "Every time a man smiles, and much more when he laughs, it adds something to his fragment of life." You need to get into the habit of saying hello to people, especially total strangers. Call people by their first name. People love to be called by name. It makes them feel important. It will make you feel better. It shows concern, friendship, zest for life, interest in people. Eventually, your smiles and handshakes will change your frame of mind and your attitude. It will make you a happier person.

Did you ever walk down a street and greet a total stranger? There are some people, especially older people, who will smile and say hi, good morning or hello. And what do you do? You smile back and say hello. You see, it's your innate nature to be kind and friendly to others. And when you treat people the way you want them to treat you, something happens.

In some cities, smiling and saying hello is really a tough thing to do. I grew up in New York City. If you say hello to someone in New York, some may think you're either out to get their money, or you're coming on to them. Smiling on the subway is almost impossible. Everyone is in a rush. Everyone seems to be late. No one looks at anyone. And everyone seems to dive for the seats, all at the same time.

William James tells us that action follows feelings. When you are happy, you think better, sleep better, and talk better. There are some people who actually cured themselves of major illness by simply laughing themselves back to health. Do me a favor and stop reading this book and smile for a few seconds. OK, how did it feel? I bet you feel better already! It is impossible to feel depressed while you are smiling. The brain cannot feel sad and happy at the same time. So smile and the whole world will smile with you.

Maintaining a happy, positive attitude is easier said than done when there is no paycheck. I need you to put into play a few important action steps that will help you along the way. These steps are outlined below.

1. Write down the specific outcome that you want. Obviously, you purchased this book with the hope of landing a job within ninety days or less. So I want you to write down the date when you fully expect to be in a new job. In addition, you need to give that date some legs. Add to that date your expected job title, income requirements and the ideal place of employment.

2. I want you to visualize what it would look like to be in this job. Try to paint some vivid pictures in your mind. They will help you to achieve your objectives.

3. Discuss your job objectives with your close friends and relatives. Tell them when you expect to get this job. Ask them if they believe you. If you can't convince them of what you want to accomplish, how can you convince your own mind? If your goal, for example, is to be a facilities manager, you need to look, sound, and talk like the best facilities manager in town. You must express confidence that this new job is right around the corner.

4. Implement an action plan that will ensure you achieve your results. I talk a little bit more about this later on.

You need to make a personal commitment as to how many phone calls, meetings, and interviews you will be going on in order to achieve your job goal.

5. During your job search activities, find time to help someone else through your unique talents. This will make you feel good and will increase your sense of self-worth.

6. Create an action stimulant that will instantly put you in a positive frame of mind. This is known as anchoring. I suggest this because depression can slowly begin to creep in over the course of unemployment.

Think of a happy moment when you were totally self-confident and were in a high state of cheerfulness. Be sure to choose an experience that you can clearly and vividly remember. Close your eyes and concentrate on this experience for a few seconds. Try to think of a movie scene which gave you the same feelings. Play these memories back and forth in your mind. When you sense you are at the height of this great feeling pinch your left thumb with your right hand. This will instantly put you in a positive frame of mind. Repeat this exercise several times until you have fully conditioned the response. Once the response is conditioned in your mind, whenever you pinch your left thumb, you will immediately feel this high state of cheerfulness.

7. Every night say a special prayer to God. Ask him for his help in securing a new job. Also let him know how you will repay him for getting that job. How you repay is entirely up to you. Just make sure you keep your promise.

Key Points

1. Getting fired can happen to anyone at any time.

2. Nurture a good sense of humor and develop a pep talk.

3. You need to convince yourself before you can convince others.

4. Develop the habit of smiling and being friendly with strangers.

5. Implement an action plan that will ensure you achieve your job objectives.

6. Anchor your positive feelings to avoid depression and put you in a positive frame of mind.

Nine

STOP WASTING YOUR TIME

"The common man is not concerned about the passage of time; the man of talent is driven by it."

- Arthur Shopenhauer

Benjamin Franklin once said, "Dost thou love life? Then do not squander time, for that is the stuff life is made of." You can get a lot accomplished when the pressure is on. Get yourself in a hurry. Do not waste or squander time. Pressure will help you avoid procrastination. You will get things accomplished. You will increase your phone calls and drive up your interview rate.

It is absolutely astounding how much time people waste. When you are about to die, what do you think you will remember the most? Believe me, it will not be some movie, restaurant, or some party you attended. You will remember the times when significant events helped to change or develop you on a very emotional level. I call these events emotional power shifts. You will remember these events as clearly as yesterday. Sometimes it takes a power shift or a memorable event to help you focus on your priorities and to make the best use of your time.

You need to cultivate those memorable events that had a positive impact on your life. They represent quantum leaps in terms of shaping your character and guiding your destiny. Let's give you one example. I once went to see *The Crucible* in New York City with my wife, Carol Ann. Martin Sheen was one of the actors in the play. As I approached the theater, I noticed Mr. Sheen outside, talking with the crowd. I thought, look at this, a major movie star, and he's taking time to talk to the crowds. What a nice thing to do. Then, after the show was over, he did it again.

After I got home, I wrote a letter to Martin Sheen. It was around Christmastime. I said I was very moved by what he had done and offered to help anyone he knew who needed a job, since I was in the recruiting business. Well, sure enough, a few weeks later, Martin Sheen came over to my office with a homeless person who needed a job.

This was an emotional power shift for me. The receptionist called me and said that Mr. Sheen was here to see me. I walked out to the lobby and sure enough, there was Martin Sheen, the famous Hollywood movie star. The Martin that I saw that day was not the actor. It was Martin, a humble soul with a giant heart. He wore a simple navy blue coat and jeans. His friend, who needed a job, was sitting next to him. He wasn't actually a friend. Martin found this man selling used magazines on Broadway in New York City. He needed a shave and his clothes were filthy. The first words I managed to blurt out were, "You got my letter!" We went to my office, where we talked about how to get this man a job.

We spent some time together. Meantime, word quickly spread around the office that Martin Sheen was on the premises, and crowds of employees started to gather outside my office. The man with the broken arm was offered a job on the condition that he pass a drug test. He subsequently failed the test and was offered a part-time job until he could clean up his act. He never returned, and I could only assume that he went back to the streets.

Due to seeing this major star of film and stage trying to help others of lesser fortune, I decided to do the same. I started conducting job search workshops for churches. I've been doing it ever since.

What does this story about Martin Sheen have to do with time? It truly helped me to focus on how I was spending my time. When we start to focus on time and how little of it we actually have, we become slightly more aware of it. Time becomes a clock that starts clicking faster and faster as we age. When we are young, we sense that we can live forever. Time is not a factor. The future seems forever. George Bernard Shaw tells us that "youth is wasted on the young." When you develop a sense of the limited amount of time that we all actually have, you tend to make better use of that time. Time becomes a very precious commodity. Awareness of time makes us want to make the most of time.

Therefore, make the most of your time and focus on those positive, emotional power shifts in your life. Think about how good it made you feel. Expand on the experience and bring it to the next level. William Shakespeare once said, "It is one of the most beautiful compensations of this life that no man can sincerely try to help another without helping himself." One way to do it is to help your community.

Some people are not inclined to give back to society until they're well on in years. It's after living a full life that they find themselves with extra time to get involved with socially redeeming activities. Although it's never too late, the time to bestow your gifts of charity is not only during your retirement years. You should do it now, especially if you're depressed or out of work. In helping others, you will help yourself. You will build your self-esteem.

Princess Diana was a shining example of this concept. She had status, fame, money, and was loved the world over. She did not have to get involved in charities, AIDS, and victims of land mines. However, she did, and at a very young age, she died in that tragic car accident in France. However, her memory and good works will last forever. So, do volunteer work in a hospital, church, charity, soup kitchen, or community center. You'll meet different and exciting people and will experience the joy of being appreciated. You will also be expanding your network. I have to tell you, there is no feeling quite like it. I guarantee it will lift your spirit and will bring you joy. And by the way, it will also make your resume look terrific.

When Martin Sheen brought the homeless person to my office, he had literally found him under a table on Broadway in New York City selling used magazines. I later found out that Martin was also involved with a soup kitchen in the

Bronx. This inspired me to get more involved with community work.

Emotional power shifts can change your course in life. They are often wake-up calls that cause you to see things in a new and different way. They are really messages from your inner self directing you to pop the clutch and turn the wheel in a different direction. You might say to yourself, why didn't I think of this sooner? What a great idea! When you have these moments in time, it is best to take massive action. These moments do not happen that often in life. For most of us, we can probably count them on our fingertips.

Key Points

1. Do not waste or squander time.

2. Cultivate those memorable events that had a positive impact on your life.

3. By helping others, you will help yourself.

4. Get involved in community work. It will bring you inner joy.

5. Emotional power shifts can change your course in life.

Ten

YOU ARE THE PRODUCT

"You can have brilliant ideas, but if you cannot get them across, your ideas will not get you anywhere."

- Lee Iacocca

The Selling of the President 1968, by Joe McGinniss, drives home the point that you are the product during a job search campaign. Nixon did not win the presidential election. His speechwriters and advertising experts put him in the White House. He was packaged and sold to the American public, lock, stock, and barrel. If you are old enough, you may recall the famous Nixon/Kennedy debates on national TV. Nixon lost that debate because he did not shave, and he refused makeup. Kennedy, on the other hand, shaved and had makeup on. He looked better and fresher than Nixon. However, most people who heard the debate on the radio thought Nixon won. Your job search is a marketing campaign, and you are the product.

When you are trying to carve out a career, it requires a lot of preparations. Resumes, networking, and interviews are all part of the career process. However, the most important thing to remember is that you will be marketing a total package. That package is you. The way you dress, speak, laugh, walk, and shake hands impacts the decision maker within the first two minutes. Your entire personality and how you project yourself ultimately will determine your success in the marketplace. Your skills are important, but skills don't initially get jobs. People who know how to project the right image get the jobs.

When you are in an interview situation, think of some good job-related stories to tell. When you interview, talk about your achievements by telling a story. Paint a vivid picture and draw upon your past. Everybody loves a storyteller. Your stories will keep your interviewer awake and interested in what you have to say. Never take yourself too seriously and try to lean on the lighter side of life. Just remember not to ramble. Keep your stories short. Make absolutely sure you have a prepared set of questions to ask during the interview. Write them down on your notepad so you don't forget to ask.

Also remember that companies don't hire resumes. Mark Twain once said, "The miracle, or the power, that elevates the few is to be found in their industry, application, and perseverance or prompting of a brave, determined spirit." If a company runs an ad, it can generate anywhere from three hundred to three thousand responses. What makes you think your resume is going to make it to the top of the selection heap? Here's the good news. The civilian labor force participation rate is currently about 65 percent. Therefore, the odds of your working are much greater than not working. In addition, with turnover ranging from 10 percent to 20 percent, millions of jobs may become available every year due to resignations and terminations. This means opportunities for you. Further, there is new job growth combined with the aging baby boomers.

The baby boomers are getting older. Several million will leave the workforce every year due to retirement. Therefore, there are virtually millions of jobs out there due to turnover, retirement, and new job growth. You just need to know and use the right strategy to find them. If you join the herd of people simply mailing out resumes, you stand a good chance of remaining unemployed or working for peanuts. Hopefully, you know by now that a savvy applicant will be more successful in finding a job than a qualified worker.

I don't care what your credentials are. You may have worked hard for your degree, but degrees don't find jobs. So do yourself a favor and avoid Resume Mountain. Now that I may have convinced you not to use your resume, I'm going to tell you how to write an award-winning resume. You see, you still need a resume. Companies and employment agencies expect you to have one. My advice to you is to avoid using them at all costs. In fact, there are only two situations when it would be advisable to present a resume. If a recruiter, headhunter, or employment agency asks you for a resume, by all means, give them one. If they are interested, they will try to sell you to their clients. The second situation is when you're in an interview and the interviewer asks you for your resume.

You also should consider getting your resume done professionally. I can't begin to tell you how many people lack the crude basics in putting a professional resume together. From the color of ink to the quality of the paper, some people just don't realize the importance of proper style and structure.

Your objective is to establish optimal eye appeal. You achieve this, in part, by using lots of white space and wide margins. Your font style should be Times New Roman or a similar common style. Your name, address, phone number, and e-mail address should appear at the top of your resume and should be in 12-point type. Many people these days leave their address off the resume to protect their identity and confidentiality. This is an overreaction. Prospective employers need to know where you live.

I am not a big believer in job summaries at the top of your resume. They usually are a lot of fluff and do nothing to capture the reader's attention. Never use a job objective. Instead, think in terms of a banner headline. The written format of your elevator pitch should be at the top of your resume. For example, Human Resources Executive with 15 Years Experience in the Pharmaceutical Industry. Following this headline should be your key skill sets using one or two words per skill set. Following the key words should be your best accomplishments that would impress your next boss. All of this belongs at the top of your resume. Everything below that should support your banner headline.

It's important to catch the reader's attention at the top one third of the page. Your resume should read like a marketing brochure. You need to dazzle the reader in the top one third of the first page. If you don't, the resume will wind up in the reject pile. Your margins should be one inch. Your paper should be 8 ½ x 11 inches, 24-pound, and with a 25 percent rag content.

You really need to use quality paper and present a professional image. A resume should be organized, sharp, clear, current, unique, and read like sales copy. Most of us are not writers by profession. We're not sales or marketing experts. That's why it is absolutely critical that after you write your resume, you have it critiqued by someone who has a flair for writing. There are many companies that specialize in resume writing. Make sure you get references and watch your budget before making any commitments.

Use the chronological format to avoid confusion. The chronological approach is the best approach. It typically organizes your resume by jobs, dates, and accomplishments. Your present and the most recent job should appear first. This is the most common acceptable format and is widely used and easy to understand. More important, it follows the same chronological approach that many executives often follow during the interview. You don't want your resume to be cute or flamboyant, unless, of course, you're interested in working in a creative field such as advertising or copywriting.

I'm not suggesting that your resume be like dull dishwater either. It is best to lean on the conservative side. There are other forms of resumes, such as the functional resume. The functional resume stresses areas that you value. These are typically skills in a variety of areas that could have been chosen from a number of different jobs you have held, such as management, quality assurance, or sales.

The problem with a functional resume is that it may appear you're hiding something. Many interviewers get very suspicious when they can't get a complete picture of your background. Listing accomplishments without dates or failing to connect them with companies can be confusing and can often causes interviewers to think the worst.

Your company and job title should be on the left side of your resume and dates of employment should be flush to the right. Any key words that support your banner headline should be bolded. If your experience is riddled with job gaps, consider using the year and omitting the day and month. Of course, you'll need to be prepared to explain the job gaps should they become an issue during the interview. If you have many years of experience, it is not necessary to go back further than twenty years. What happened twenty years ago is most likely not relevant.

Always highlight your company's financial stats. You want to include a short financial overview of your present or last company. It should be a separate paragraph after the company's geographic information. This will demonstrate that you are knowledgeable about your company, are sensitive to costs, appreciate numbers, and can see the big picture.

Why should a company consider hiring you? Companies couldn't care less about "tombstone resumes" containing vital statistics, references, schools attended, report cards, or what your job objectives are. You need to base your written and verbal remarks in terms of what the employer objectives are. Companies are not charities put on this earth to give you a handout.

You should have a minimum of three but no more than five accomplishments for every job you ever held. We're not looking for a few base hits. We're talking homers, touchdowns, and grand slammers! Your accomplishments should explode with vitality! When a recruiter or executive reads your accomplishments, it should make him or her feel like it's the Fourth of July. I'm going to show you how to write dynamite accomplishments that will cause fireworks when your accomplishments are read. Every accomplishment should start with an action verb. You need to put drama and passion into your achievements. Every accomplishment should tell what you did. However, whatever you did, it needs to be relevant to the company you want to work for.

Every accomplishment should also indicate how much you did. Companies live and die based on what occurs at the bottom line. What you don't want to do is blurt out how you accomplished your magnificent achievements. You should save these juicy details for the interview. You want to wet the company's appetite and sell the sizzle. If you give them the complete recipe, they may not invite you to the dinner.

You want to use tight, crisp, concise statements and get straight to the point. Do not brag or boast. Make no value judgments. Let the facts speak for themselves. The ideal accomplishments indicate money saved in terms of actual dollars, time, or effort. If you don't have a lot of job accomplishments under your belt, think of accomplishments in schools, charities, trade associations, sports, etc.

Consider joining two professional or trade associations. Regardless of what you do, there is probably a trade or professional association that is relevant to your type of work. Go to the library and ask for the *Directory of Associations*. There are over fifty thousand associations in the United States with membership directories. You should join at least two associations. One association should be directly related to your line of work. The second association does not have to be related to your line of work, but should have a crosslink. Consider joining an organization that your next boss may belong to.

I encourage this approach for several reasons. The unrelated association is useful because the people that you will network with are not competing for the same jobs. In addition, belonging to different associations increases the breadth and scope of your resume. You want to paint an image of someone with many skills and talents. Thirdly, it will do wonders for your networking.

When joining organizations of any kind, you need to take a good look at the benefits versus the membership fees. A critical factor is whether or not the association has a local chapter. If there is no local chapter, choose another association that does have a local chapter. You need to get your money's worth from these associations. Go to monthly meetings and become involved in your association. Volunteer for one of the committees. This is give and take. If you just join the association to further your career without helping the members, it defeats the whole purpose of joining. You absolutely do not want to join an association just for the express purpose of finding work.

If you decide to join an association, make sure you put it on your resume. However, remember, your skills, my friend, are more important than your education or any association to which you belong. I'm not suggesting that a college degree is not a useful selling point on your resume. A degree will certainly put you miles ahead of the high school crowd. And if you're in a top-rated school and have a terrific grade point average, that's even better. However, keep in mind that these credentials are more important to the big companies and the big institutions and less important to the smaller companies which do most of the hiring.

Small companies will hire and pay you more for your skills. Think about it. A degree in economics or business is not going to help you create Excel spreadsheets or PowerPoint presentations. It will not teach you how to produce an operations manual that everyone can read and understand. However, if, on day one, you can do any of these things, that's a useful skill to have.

You should know by now that while resumes may not unlock the door to opportunities, they can play a vital role in the job search process. If you target a company and customize your resume for that company, it will help.

Key Points

1. Your job search is a marketing campaign and you are the product.

2. When you interview, talk about your achievements by telling a story.

3. The retiring baby boomers will create millions of job openings.

4. Avoid being interviewed over the phone.

5. Get your resume done by a professional. It's worth the investment.

6. Companies are not charities put on this earth to give you a handout.

7. Consider joining two professional or trade associations.

Eleven

HOW TO TAKE THE WORK OUT OF NETWORKING

"Poverty, I realized, wasn't only a lack of financial resources. It was isolation from the kind of people that could help you make more of yourself."

- Keith Ferrazzi

I was once asked to join a team to help out in planning some networking events. My position to the team was that most networking events are like going to work. People don't want to work after work. They want to have fun. So I developed this concept called "stealth networking." You actually get to know people—a lot of people—and you're having a lot of fun in the process. People don't realize they are networking because they're having so much fun. That's the way it should be. Whenever you go to a networking event, please go to have fun and make some friends. The business talk will come naturally.

Networking, according to Webster's dictionary, is "the developing of contacts or exchanging of information with others in an informal network, as to further career." It is a mutual, cooperative endeavor. It is something that our species started in the early beginnings of mankind in an effort to survive. According to research by Robert W. Sussman, professor of anthropology at Washington University in St. Louis, our intelligence and cooperation are features we developed to outsmart predators. Networking is a form of cooperation that comes very naturally to all us. The challenge is that some people are better at it than others. If we were not good at it when walking with the Neanderthals, then our ancestors probably ran the risk of becoming dinner for some saber-toothed tiger. Have things really changed that much today? I don't think so.

Networking personally helped me in my job search endeavors. When I secured a position as a speech writer and training director, I obtained that position through a college professor. On another occasion, I landed a job as a vice president of human resources because I knew the decision maker from a former company. I picked up the phone and made a call. In both of these situations, I had a casual, working relationship. They knew me and were willing to either refer or hire me.

Ralph Waldo Emerson, American poet and essayist, once said, "The only way to have a friend is to be one." The average person looking for a job these days will scan the Internet and surf the major job boards. According to most surveys, only 20 percent of all job openings are advertised through the want ads. The remaining 80 percent are never advertised. People find out about these jobs through networking. I'm not suggesting that you ignore the job boards. Your job search needs to be multidimensional. However, you do need to recognize that job postings can generate hundreds of responses from people looking for jobs. Human resources directors, recruiters, and executives sift through their stacks of resumes at lightning speed. Believe me, as a vice president of human resources, I know what it is like to riffle through three hundred resumes in a nanosecond.

You may have spent hours preparing your resume. It may have cost you a considerable sum of money to make it look really professional. You may even think you have the best résumé in town. And I hope you do! However, that recruiter, executive, or human resource director doesn't really care about how much time or money you plowed into your resume. If you're lucky, your resume will be looked at for about fifteen seconds. If the right phrase, tone, or message doesn't jump off that piece of paper, you're history. And don't count on a rejection letter, because most companies won't take the time to send you one.

If you want to find a job these days, you need to become an aggressive job hunter. If you take the passive approach by only mailing out resumes, you will miss out on the majority of job opportunities. Some experts suggest you do a mass mailing. In fact, there are some organizations that will do this for you for a fee. You will be lucky if you get a 1 percent response rate. It is not worth your time or money. To find a job, you absolutely need to include networking. It's not what you know, it's who you know. It's called connections, pull, politics, influence, the inside track, pulling strings, carrying weight, and knowing the power behind the throne.

Networking is a highly organized system of meeting, communicating, and helping people in the spirit of cooperation.

It includes your doing someone a favor with the unexpected reward of having someone return the favor. Networking is a two-way street. If you attempt to uncover job openings while networking in professional organizations without helping others in the network, you will be doing a disservice to your network. People will see you coming a mile away.

Now, if your attitude is that you don't have time to network, I would encourage you not to network. You have to remember that networking is a long-term commitment. Your goal is to develop friendships and business relationships that will, perhaps, last a lifetime.

How do you begin to establish your network? First, you need to compile a list of everyone you know, including friends, relatives, business associates, acquaintances, members of your church or synagogue, doctors, dentists, associations, etc. It's important to organize your contacts. Using Excel is one way to maintain your contact list and keep it up to date. It should include names, phone numbers, e-mail addresses, names of referrals received, and date last contacted. Once you have established a network, your job search will be cut significantly. Organizing and tracking your network is really important.

While we are on the subject of networking, I strongly urge you to join LinkedIn.com. This is a free web site (although you can buy upgrades) with well over seventy million users. I can practically develop an organizational chart of a company by using LinkedIn. It is a great way to connect with other professionals and learn about different companies and job openings. LinkedIn also has various groups that you can join that may be related to your specialty. You can develop your profile on LinkedIn, and in time you can develop a network in the thousands!

It is important to note that once you start to cultivate your network, it will expand through referrals. It is highly likely that your next job will be secured through someone you don't know yet. Let me explain.

In May 1973, the *American Journal of Sociology* published "The Strength of Weak Ties." It was written by Mark Granovetter. This paper is considered to be a landmark study in sociology. Weak ties, defined as "casual acquaintances," are more valuable in securing employment than strong ties. Why is this? Strong ties make up only a minority percentage of networking contacts. Weak ties provide more job leads because they involve less risk and a lower level of trust about the competency of the individual.

Networking is as old as mankind. People have always sought the help of other people when a need developed. It has gained enormous popularity today as a job search technique due to the enormous number of people who are finding it really difficult to land a job. The key is to know how to network. It will serve you well to follow these simple rules when attending group meetings with networking opportunities:

1. Arrive early and stay late.
2. Spend three to five minutes with each person.

3. Give a firm handshake.
4. Seek ways to help those you meet.
5. Don't prejudge people.
6. Bring your business cards.

At all costs, avoid asking self-serving questions. Dale Carnegie once said, "You can make more friends in two minutes by taking an interest in others than in two years trying to get other people interested in you."

Once you start to consciously network, you will start to meet a lot of people. There is absolutely no way that you are going to remember the names of everyone you meet unless you devise a system. As soon as you meet someone and that person becomes a part of your network, you need to enter the name into a log book, Rolodex, or database. If you don't write it down, you will forget the conversation. This information will become critical in future communications. You need to record when and where you met the person and the name of the person who introduced you (if that was the case). Try to write down something about the person's appearance that will help you to remember him or her. It will also be helpful to jot down the major topic if the meeting took place at a seminar or trade association, etc. Above all, remember the person's name and call that person by name when you see him or her again.

Make sure you have business cards. I don't care if you're working or not working. You must have a business card. And don't leave home without it! You cannot properly network without a business card. And it doesn't matter if you are a cook, waitress, bartender, or mail clerk. All great professional networkers have business cards. If you're not working, your business card should have your name, job specialty, address, and phone number on it. If you don't have a phone, hook up with an answering service or use the phone number of a relative. Many interviews fall through the cracks because recruiters can't make contact with the applicants by phone and move on to the next candidate. Never volunteer your business card. Instead, within the first ten minutes ask the person you are speaking with for his or her business card. Usually that person will then ask you for your card.

Keep in mind that you are developing business relationships, which may develop into friendships. Relationships require time in order to develop. I'm not suggesting that you eventually need to be the best of friends with everyone in your network. I am saying that you need to develop rapport with your network so when the time comes to ask for help, your network will respond if they can. That being said, you should never ask for a job. Instead, ask for a referral. If you ask for a job, chances are that person will not have a job for you and the door shuts. If you simply ask for a referral, the door remains open. You get into referral discussions once you start talking about your targeted company list. Under no circumstances should you come across as someone who is self-serving. You must show genuine interest, concern, and respect for your network, because if you don't, your network will not work.

Learn how to break the ice. If you're the shy type, get over it really quickly. It can mean the difference between unemployment and a thriving career. When you first meet a stranger, introduce yourself with a firm handshake and a pleasant smile. Make eye contact. Don't wait for someone to approach you. Pick out someone who is older and therefore more experienced than you. Walk right up to the person and introduce yourself.

If you're the shy type, bring a friend along as a guest. There is safety in numbers. Once you exchange names, a great way to break the ice is to ask a question. The trick is to ask an open-ended question that requires an answer other than yes or no. A really good question is one that asks for advice, because it will make the person feel important. Here are some good examples of what questions you can ask:

1. I'm kind of new to this association. What's a good way to get more involved?
2. Tonight's topic concerns benefits. What do you think we'll gain from this session?
3. What do you do?
4. How did you first start with your company?
5. What's the biggest challenge this year in your organization?
6. Why did you come to this meeting?
7. Where do you see your company heading during the next twelve months?

What do you notice about these questions? The focus is not on you and your need to find a job. The focus is on the person you are talking with. Find ways to help the person you are talking with.

When the discussion turns to you, focus on these two important topics:

1. Your elevator speech.
2. Your marketing plan.

Your elevator speech is important because you need people to understand what you're looking for. If they don't know what you're looking for, it will be difficult for them to help you or even provide you with the right referrals. Your marketing plan shows your target list of companies. In fact, you will want to give people a copy of your marketing plan for future reference and follow-up calls. Here is a sample elevator speech:

> "For the last five years, I was a director of purchasing for XYZ company. While there, I established a state-of-the-art inventory system and reduced copier equipment costs by 35 percent. This is my target list of companies I would like to work for. Do you happen to know anyone who works for any of these companies? If yes, would you mind if I used your name as a referral? Can you think of any companies I should add to this list?"

Your goal is to become a referred employee. It begins with meeting people and sharing your target companies list. Your goal is to contact someone in your target companies through a referral. Your ultimate goal is to make contact with your next boss in those targeted companies. Your skill sets take a back seat to referrals every time.

When you're talking to people, always try to smile, listen, and maintain a positive attitude. It's important to make people feel comfortable and to enjoy the experience. The best way to do this is to smile. It costs nothing, it's painless, it will put you in a positive frame of mind, and you'll feel and look better. The person you're talking to will see your smile, and it will leave a favorable impression. You also need to be an active listener. You can do this with your eyes, by nodding your head, and by using words or phrases that project understanding: "I see," "Uh-huh," "Interesting."

Never end a conversation without sharing your target companies list and getting a referral. It is amazing, but people who are less qualified and know someone get the job faster than people who are more qualified but with no contacts. People do not like to hire strangers. Companies prefer to hire people through referrals or recommendations. Companies will pay their employees for referrals. If the choice is between a referred person and a stranger, the referred person has an edge even though he or she may be less qualified.

Most jobs are filled long before they hit the want ads through the employee referral process. Your network may include friends and acquaintances whose companies have job openings. Find out about these openings and ask your contact if you can use his or her name. Names open up doors like magic. Corporations in the United States spend over $20 million a year on employee referrals. Why will many companies spend anywhere between $200 and $3,000 per referral? The answer is that all of us were brought up with the idea that we should not associate with strangers. Companies want to feel comfortable before they put you on their payroll. After all, as soon as you become an employee, you are automatically endowed with special rights or privileges, depending upon the state where you live.

Companies don't want to take chances. They are not just hiring you. They are incurring a multitude of expenses, such as worker's compensation, unemployment taxes, payroll taxes, health insurance, life insurance, new hire costs, and the list goes on, depending upon the benefits package of the particular company.

Stay in touch with your network. If you don't stay in touch with your network, your network will dry up. After meeting someone for the first time, send a short note within two weeks and briefly comment on the meeting. If possible, include a sincere compliment. Instead of asking for a job, send an article from a newspaper or magazine which you think may be of interest to the person. Make a copy of the article so you can refer to it when you speak to him or her again. Your strategy here is to give instead of take. Get in the habit of calling your contacts every three to four weeks. Try to share information that will be valuable to them. Do breakfast or lunch. Remember, you're developing relationships that may last a lifetime.

Key Points

1. Smart people find out about job openings through networking.

2. Weak ties are better than strong ties in uncovering job leads.

3. Never leave home without your business cards.

4. Bring along copies of your marketing plan. Show it to your contacts and obtain referrals.

5. Never ask for a job; always ask for a referral.

6. If you're shy when it comes to networking, bring a friend.

7. Focus on the person you are talking with and not your need for a job.

8. Smile, listen, and maintain a positive attitude.

9. One of your main goals is to become a referral and eventually make contact with your next boss.

10. Maintain a contact directory, including name, phone, e-mail, last date contacted, and names of referrals.

11. Join LinkedIn.com.

12. Stay in touch with your network.

Twelve

SMILE, DIAL, AND MAKE THE PHONE YOUR BEST FRIEND

"I don't answer the phone. I get the feeling whenever I do that there will be someone on the other end."

- Fred Couples

This chapter explains exactly what you need to do to launch an effective job search campaign with the goal of landing a new job within the first ninety days. There are basically eight elements to launch your campaign as shown below. The most critical part of your campaign is to make use of the phone. If you rely solely on mailing letters, the results will be disappointing.

1. Research
2. Elevator Pitch
3. Resume
4. Marketing Plan
5. Networking
6. Mailing Letters
7. Job Boards
8. Phone Calls

Launching a job campaign, in many ways, is like launching a new product or service. Job search contains many of the same elements of sales, marketing, advertising, and public relations. The number one rule to remember is this: You must at all times maintain a full pipe line. The basis of this advice is simple. Just like sales people can't rely on a few cold calls to consistently close many deals, you can't rely on a few contacts to get your next job. You can't put all of your eggs in one basket like responding to job postings on-line. You need to prime the pump through people contact. Ideally, you will have multiple job offers in your pipeline. This way, you can make the best choice based on your purpose, passion, preferences, talent, and long-term life goals. You really don't want to settle for the first job that comes along. This may be very difficult to do when the mortgage or rent has to be paid. However, if you conduct your job search the right way, you will have a choice regarding which job offer to accept.

Launching an effective job search campaign also means knowing how much time to spend on your techniques. Passive job hunters who spend countless hours in front of their computer sending resumes to cyberspace have their heads in the clouds. This is not making the best use of your time. Most of your time must be spent meeting and talking with people. This is why job search is so difficult for many people. They are not wired to do this. Many are reserved and introverted. However, to land a job quickly will require most of you to get out of your comfort zone. You will need to get uncomfortable and stretch your limits. Look at it from this perspective: The faster you get through it, the faster you will be employed again.

Research

You can't develop your elevator pitch until you know what industries and companies you want to work for. This will require some research. Job search requires a lot of thought. Would you prefer to work for a hospital or a restaurant? If it's a service provider, what type of service is it? Is it cars, phones, computers, software or garbage disposal? Your decision regarding what industries and companies you want to work for will be linked to your purpose, passion, preferences, and talents. Give it some thought. Do your research. Figure out what kind of company will make you happy. One of my first jobs after high school was working for a clothing manufacturer in Queens, New York. I had to walk around the shop floor with a stop watch and clip board and determine how long it would take the workers to perform their tasks. I absolutely hated this job and quit after two days. I learned that working in the apparel industry was not my dream job. Do what you love and love what you do. Follow this advice and you will become an extremely valuable employee for any company you choose to work for.

Your research should also involve choosing a growth industry versus a declining industry. Industries that are growing will generally provide better pay, benefits and promotional opportunities. Growth industries are generally more fun to work for. Declining industries are cutting benefits and perks, and you eventually may be downsized when they go through their next round of job cuts. It can also be very depressing working for a company that's sliding down hill.

Depending on the industry and the job position you are seeking, it may become necessary to broaden your list of industries and companies. To maintain a full pipeline of job possibilities, you need to determine the number of positions available in your industry and companies of choice. The number of actual job openings is irrelevant. Chances are, when you contact companies, they will not have a job waiting for you. This is why you need a full pipeline. Job search is a numbers and timing game. To make my system work, you need to have a minimum of two hundred positions in your industries and companies. Thus, if you are a chief financial officer and you identified thirty companies in one industry and each company in that industry has one chief financial officer, then you have identified thirty positions. You need at least 200 positions. In this case, you would either have to expand the number of companies in your industry and location or expand the number of industries and locations where you would like to work. Having just thirty positions will not pass the pipeline test.

Also, part of your research will require identifying the name of your future boss. This is critical. You need to eventually connect with the person who has the power and authority to hire you. It is not a recruiter or some other middle person in the hierarchy. It is your next boss. Get his or her name and job title. Make sure you know how to pronounce his or her name properly. Find out what associations he/she belongs to and join those associations. You eventually want to get referred to your next boss, if possible. If this is not possible, then you will need to make direct contact through a targeted, well-written letter and follow-up with a phone call. We'll talk about phone techniques a little later in this chapter.

By the way, be flexible on where you want to work. Most people over the age of forty are usually not moving away from their current city. They have their roots established. Younger people tend to be more flexible. There are many cities with very high unemployment. There are also many cities with very low unemployment. Depending on the job you are seeking, you will much more likely find employment where the unemployment is low. You can easily find this information on-line through the U.S. Bureau of Labor Statistics (www.bls.gov). Do your homework!

What size and type of company do you want to work for? Do those companies hire people with your skills and talents? Where does your company need to be located? Would you prefer to work in your current city or are you open to relocation? What kind of culture does your ideal company have? Would it be for profit or nonprofit, public or private? Are your target companies financially solvent? Is the industry you targeted a growing industry? What is the competition like for your job where you live? Do you need to consider other locations where there is less competition and higher demand for the work that you do? When I moved from New York City to Atlanta, I accomplished several things: (1) new job with more pay, (2) a new house with lower taxes, and (3) got to live in a warmer climate. Along the way, I wrote a book and became part-owner of a high-growth company. I followed my gut instincts and took massive action.

How you go about conducting your research is not that difficult. First of all, you have access to the internet and can find a ton of information about industries and companies for free. Check out the company's web site and use Google or other search engines to find out information about your target companies and the people who work for those companies. Another free resource is the research librarian in your local library. He or she will be more than happy to help you. Your first stop is the reference section. Ask the librarian for help. Most libraries will have directories by Hoovers, and Dun and Bradstreet. The Book of Lists is another excellent source. You have two goals when conducting this research:

1. Find out as much as you can about the company.
2. Identify your next boss.

You may not be able to identify your next boss through your research. Through a combination of networking and phone calls, you will eventually get the names. Think like a detective. Here's one quick tip: Try calling the company and simply ask who has responsibility over the department where you want to work. Also get the correct spelling of the name and job title.

The Elevator Pitch

Before you even begin to think about writing your resume, mailing letters or calling your contacts, you need to develop your elevator pitch. Your elevator pitch is basically a very concise summary of what you do, what makes you special and two to three accomplishments that support your pitch. In sales, this is commonly known as your opening paragraph. You have less than ten seconds to grab your listener's or reader's interest. Whatever you say or do, you cannot come across as someone who is asking for a job. If you do, the interest level will diminish very quickly. You want to avoid putting people on the defensive. The written version of your pitch will appear at the top of your resume. Everything else on your resume will support your pitch. When you are networking, it is your pitch that will flow off your tongue to impress and interest the person you are talking to. Your pitch is your banner headline. It defines who you are and what you want to do today. Your pitch will impact your referral rate.

A good portion of this book encourages you to factor in your purpose, passion, preferences, and talents with your job objectives. I hammer this point home again and again. In order for you to achieve maximum fulfillment in life, your job and your purpose must be in sync. If they are not in sync, you will be out of balance and, quite frankly, you will not live to your full potential. Let's assume that you have worked on your purpose, passion, preferences, and talents and finally figured out your calling in life. Now you are ready to develop your pitch because you did the research and know exactly what you want to do and where you want to work. People cannot help you unless they know exactly what you are looking for in terms of career objectives. You need to help them help you. Always remember, most people are more than happy to help if they can. You just need to show them the way.

Keep in mind that the length of your pitch may vary depending upon the circumstances. Common sense and respect for the person's time should always be your guide. You are striving to be concise, succinct and to the point. You don't want to sound like you are boasting about your accomplishments, yet you do need to get across the key things you are most proud of. Try to make your pitch sound conversational. Here is one example of a good elevator pitch.

Sample Elevator Pitch

I'm a chief operating officer with 15 years experience in the waste and recycling industry. In fact, last year the National Recycling Association presented me with an award for an innovative recycling program I launched resulting in reducing recycling costs for my company by 25%.

Some of my major areas of expertise include waste and recycling, profit and loss management, procurement and sustainability. During my last engagement with XYZ Corporation, a major 500 company, I expanded the client recycling volume by 45% resulting in over two million in rebate income. I also was successful in increasing corporate revenues by 34% over a two-year period.

The Resume

We already covered the components of a good resume. Unless you're a gifted writer, I recommend you have it done professionally and avoid the risk of losing job opportunities because your resume was poorly written. Your resume needs to read like you are the perfect candidate for the job you're seeking. Your resume should be somewhat personal and filled with interesting facts and accomplishments that support your elevator pitch. It needs to read like a marketing brochure. Many people these days don't even put their home address on their cover letter or resume due to identity theft concerns. This is overkill. Prospective employers want to know where you live and you should include this information. If you're concerned about identity theft, there are plenty of organizations that can help protect you. Do not focus on the activities when writing accomplishments. Focus on the results. Employers don't care about the minutia involved in getting the job done. They want to know the bottom line. What was the outcome? How much money did you save? How fast did your new strategy get the job done? Do not bore them with the details. Sell the sizzle, not the steak. Save the meaty details for the interview. While you do need a well-crafted resume and cover letter, please keep in mind that the resume and cover letter will not get you the job. It is your communication skills and your ability to expand your referral rate that will eventually land you your job.

The Marketing Plan

Most job hunters I talk to do not have a marketing plan. Yet, your marketing plan is the single, most important document in your job search tool box. It is even more important than your resume. A well-crafted marketing plan will show the written version of your elevator pitch at the top. Below your elevator pitch should be four to eight major skill sets. Following your skill sets should be your top three accomplishments and your list of industries and the specific companies you have targeted. Why is this so important? When you talk to people, you are not going to be asking them for a job. I know this sounds crazy. You're looking for a job and I'm telling you not to ask for a job. Chances are they will not have a job for you. If you ask for a job and they don't have one, the conversation is over. Your goal is to become a referral. Your initial objective is to share your marketing plan with the people you talk to. The most important question you will be asking is this: Do you know anyone on my list that works for any of these companies? If the answer is yes, then your second question is to find out if the person would be willing to recommend you to the company. A recommendation is worth its weight in gold. Companies prefer to hire someone they know through a referral than someone they don't know from Adam. Even if the referred candidate is less qualified, they have a better shot at getting the job.

Who should you share your marketing plan with? The answer is everyone: Your dentist, doctor, friends, relatives, neighbors, business associates, church or synagogue and fellow members of associations.

Obviously, you can't produce a marketing plan until you complete your research. Once you have identified the companies you want on your plan, make it your business to know those companies inside out. This will require study and analysis. The payoff comes when you are talking with the decision-maker and it is obvious that you did your homework.

Networking

I have already devoted a whole chapter to networking. The important point I want to stress here is that you need to focus on the person you are talking with and not your need to get a job. It is all about developing relationships. People will help you if they like you. How do you get people to like you? You get people to like you by taking an interest in them. If you are in a networking meeting, you should be asking questions about the person you're talking to and not your marketing plan. Your marketing plan will come up later. First develop the relationship by taking an interest in the person you are talking to. Once you break the ice by taking an interest, then you can bring up your marketing plan. Avoid talking about your needs up front. In fact, don't even use the word "I" during your initial conversation. It should be all about the other person. Try to take a genuine interest in other people and look for ways to help them. People generally respond in kind.

Your main objective while networking is to figure out how you can do this person a favor. It could be something as simple as sending a relevant magazine article or providing information about his or her industry that he/she may not be privy to. Once you help that person, he or she will be more willing to help you. The help you are looking for is to get a referral. Once this relationship has been established, you need to keep the relationship alive especially if this person could offer you a job if one existed. Remember, I mentioned it is a timing game. This month, your contact may not have a job for you. But next month can be a very different picture. You must contact your network every three to four weeks. When you call or send an email, it needs to always be upbeat, even though you still are not employed. People do not generally like to associate with people who are depressed and complaining all the time. So remain upbeat and send them another relevant article if you can. Your contacts need to remember you and they need to know you are still in the game. Help them help you.

Networking can be very slow. Attending the monthly meeting is good, but chances are you will not be gainfully employed within ninety days by attending three meetings. You must accelerate your search by targeted mail and phone calls. Writing letters and making phone calls is a full-time job. This is hard work, especially if you're not used to doing it. Your hard work and efforts will pay off when you get your first paycheck from your new employer.

Mailing Letters

You need to prepare a well-crafted letter and send it to a specific person in the company you want to work for. This person may be your next boss. This letter must be personalized. It can't be one of the hundreds of letters that will wind up in the trash can. Use a large envelope so you don't have to fold your letter. Hand-write the address and use a blue, felt-tip pen. Use postage stamps instead of metered stamps. You don't want to appear to be just another job hunter.

Your letter needs to establish a bond of familiarity. It could be a weak connection through a school, college, association or someone you know that knows someone in your targeted company. You accomplish this by either mentioning the name of someone who may work for the company or perhaps is a member of an association that your next boss is a member of. If you can establish even a remote connection with your next boss through either a mutual acquaintance or an association, it will open up doors. The most critical part of your mail campaign is to follow-up with a phone call. In fact, the last line in your letter should state that you will be following up with the person in a few days. Failure to make the follow-up call is the kiss of death. It will clearly demonstrate that you do not keep your commitments. By the way, don't be surprised if the person you are calling does not recall reading your letter. Decision-makers tend to get a lot of mail. Sometimes you may get lucky when the person receiving your letter actually calls you. Of course, you need to make sure your cell number is on your letter. When the phone rings, answer it. Do not let it go to voice mail. You may not get a second shot.

If you cannot establish a bond of familiarity with your targeted company, you can still write them a letter. The big difference here is that you will have a lower success rate. However, you will still need to mount a mail campaign with or without a connection because your goal is to have a full pipeline of potential employers.

Job Boards

Job seekers can and do get jobs through job boards. The problem is that a very small percentage of people are successful in getting jobs this way. The reason is pretty simple. You are competing with hundreds of other job seekers for the same job! Most companies will not even acknowledge that they received your resume. This can be extremely frustrating. My recommendation is that you do not spend hours and hours in front of your computer sending your resume to the clouds. Instead, devote perhaps one hour per day on the job boards. In addition, do your research and try to identify the decision maker on those posted jobs. If successful in doing this, you can send a targeted letter to the decision maker and avoid the cattle drive.

Phone Calls

Most salespeople hate to make cold calls, but readily admit that if they do not make cold calls, there will be no sales and no commissions. Let's face it, who feels like calling some stranger and striking up a conversation? If you don't have an outgoing personality, it will be difficult for you to make a cold call. It's no wonder that only a small percentage of the population makes a living in sales. My philosophy in landing a job in ninety days or less is not about making cold calls, and you don't have to be an extrovert. It is all about making warm calls. The point is that you absolutely must pick up the phone and call people you may not know as well as those you do know. If you have a fear of picking up the phone, I will help you get over your problem. So what can possibly motivate you to pick up the phone and make a call? The answer is ninety days! This book, in case you forgot, is all about getting a great job in 90 days or less.

We have already talked about networking. I consider networking soft job hunting. Really, anyone can do it. Networking occurs in various ways. It could occur in a room with a large group of people. You strike up a conversation and eventually it will lead to you talking about your job search activities. Networking can occur in other situations as well. It could be at the dentist's office or perhaps having lunch with a couple of business acquaintances. It could occur through a phone call to a friend or acquaintance.

Networking is very different than cold calling. Unless you are calling a network buddy, most networking generally takes more time and is often not on your schedule. You are often working on someone else's schedule. For example, professional organizations usually meet once a month. When you attend these meetings, you will not be able to network effectively with everyone. There is simply not enough time. Getting a job in ninety days or less will generally not happen through traditional networking simply because it takes a long time to network your way into a new job. If an organization has meetings once a month, you will only have three opportunities to land a job within ninety days given one meeting per month. At that pace, I can guarantee you will not find a new job within ninety days. Am I suggesting that you do not network? Of course not! Networking is a powerful way to secure contacts and eventually get that next job. The problem is that it is a slow process and your contacts are limited.

Time is not on your side. You need to speed the process up. This is where my system and philosophy come into play.

Using the phone will accelerate your job search in ways you cannot imagine. How you go about using the phone in a job search is an art that you will have to master. I will tell you how to do it. I realize you may not be a salesperson. Here is the good news: neither am I! Yet, I have secured jobs using these techniques, so I know that they work. We are at a point now in this book where you hopefully have a pretty good idea of the philosophy I have been talking about. This philosophy is not just about your finding a job. It is about taking a deep look inside yourself in an effort to connect your passion, preferences, compassion, goals, action, and purpose to what you do for a living. I've mentioned my philosophy before. It's worth mentioning again:

Your passion, purpose, talent, and preferences need to be in alignment with your chosen profession.

Living a purposeful and compassionate life will lead to self-fulfillment.

Ultimately, you are seeking self-fulfillment and a no-regrets life. You need to focus on the bigger picture. As an earthling, you need to be working really hard to secure a place in this world. It is probably difficult for most people to think in these terms. Most people, I guess, probably try to live a decent life and hope for the best after they are gone. I'm asking you to try and see the big picture. Life is not just about working and paying the rent. You are a unique individual and you are here for a purpose. It is your duty to seek this purpose out and fulfill it. When you get to the job phase of this philosophy, you must know what you want to do and where you want to work. You will need to start making at least ten phone calls a day or fifty phone calls per week. I can hear you right now. Are you out of your mind! Am I working in some kind of call center? I can't make that number of phone calls. It's too hard. I feel uncomfortable. Let's you and I have a talk. I am asking you to get out of your comfort zone. If you believe in the ancient, advanced civilizations, do you think they were out of their comfort zone when they accomplished the monoliths centuries ago? I never said this would be easy. The question that you need to ask yourself is this: do I want a job within ninety days or would I prefer to wait two years? It's your call. You can do this. If we can put men on the moon, you can make a simple phone call. You need to get in survival mode. Your long-term financial security depends on it!

I mentioned before that job search is, in many ways, a number game. It's about keeping your pipeline full. Your use of the phone will involve a combination of follow-up calls based on your mail campaign and warm calls to people you already know. The key to a successful job search is consistency. You need to get into the habit of making calls on a daily basis. Ideally, you will know the night before exactly who you will be calling on the next day. Your phone calls will include follow-up calls based on your mail campaign and making direct calls not proceeded by a letter. Here is how one scenario might work out:

Ninety Days to a New Job Requires a Full Pipeline

- 10 calls per day, 50 calls per week
- 12 weeks x 50 calls = 600 calls within 90 days

As I have mentioned before, this is a numbers game and you have to keep the pipeline full. The question is: Who do you call and what do you say? Your guide will be your marketing plan. After your research is completed, you will have identified the industries and companies with at least two hundred positions that are a match for the job you are seeking. You have already started to identify referrals in these organizations. You have already started your mail campaign. You should have a daily list of people to call.

I mentioned earlier that you will be making warm calls and not cold calls. What is the difference between these kinds of calls? A cold call is when you are calling someone you don't know and have no referral to facilitate the conversation. A warm call is when you either have a referral or the name of a person, group, or association that is readily known by the person you wish to speak with. Your objective is to create a sense of familiarity so the person feels more comfortable in speaking with you. Let me repeat that phrase: a sense of familiarity. This one piece of advice is worth its weight in gold. Please trust me and take it to heart.

Here is a sample dialogue when your referral permits you to use his or her name in calling someone:

You: "Hi, Mike, this is Ron Williams. Sarah Hillman referred me to you. Do you know Sarah?

Contact: "Yes, I do."

You: "Great. Sarah speaks very highly of you and suggested you might be able to help me out regarding my networking activities. Did you receive the letter I sent to you?

Contact: "Yes."

You: "Great. Did I catch you at a bad time?"

Contact: "No. This is fine."

You: "Mike, I worked for five years as a purchasing director for XYZ company. I was instrumental in launching a state-of-the-art inventory system and reduced their copier costs by 35 percent.

As you know, networking is critical in finding job opportunities. I have a list of target companies I have an interest in. Would you be willing to take a look at this list and let me know if you know of anyone who may be employed by one of these companies?"

Contact: "Ron, I'd be happy to take a look at your list. Can you e-mail it to me?"

You: "Absolutely. And Mike, would it be possible for us to meet in a week or two for perhaps fifteen minutes? It's always good to put a name with a face.

Contact: "Not a problem, Ron."

Then you proceed to set a date for the meeting. When you send the contact your targeted company list, also send your resume and an article you think he or she may have an interest in. Since people respond in kind, the article will provide another incentive for your contact to give you referrals. You should also strive to get your contact to allow you to use his or her name when you are talking to his or her referrals. Using a name is priceless.

What do you do if you don't have a referral to mention during the conversation? You can try using an association or other group reference that either the person is a member of or at least knows of the association or the group.

It is in your interest to find out what associations or groups your next boss may be a member of.

In the dialogue below, you know the contact is a member of the association because you have the membership directory. You have access to the membership directory because you joined that association. You will need to belong to at least two professional associations in order to get enough contacts in your pipeline. However, do not limit your mailings and warm calls to members of professional associations. There are many, many groups that you can tap into.

Here's a sample dialogue when you don't have a referral:

You: "Hi, Mike. This is Ron Williams. I'm a fellow member of the International Association of Purchasing Professionals. Did you receive the letter I sent to you?"

Contact: "Yes, I did."

You: "Great. Did I catch you at a bad time?"

Contact: "No, this is fine."

You: Mike, I worked for five years as a purchasing director for XYZ company. I was instrumental in launching a state-of-the-art inventory system and reduced their copier costs by 35 percent.

As you know, networking is critical in finding job opportunities. Several members of the association have already provided me with some valuable help.

I have a list of target companies I have an interest in. Would you be willing to take a look at this list and let me know if you know of anyone who may be employed by one of these companies?"

Contact: "Ron, I'd be happy to take a look at your list. Can you e-mail it to me?"

You: "Absolutely. And Mike, would it be possible for us to meet in a week or two for perhaps fifteen minutes? It's always good to put a name with a face.

Contact: "Not a problem, Ron."

Then proceed to set a date for your meeting. If you can establish some kind of bond with contacts, such as being fellow members of a common association, that is worth its weight in gold. People will talk to you because you have a bond of familiarity. Your contact is familiar with the association or group and will happily help a fellow member. He or she might even run into you at some future meeting and would not want to be looked upon negatively because they did not help you. More importantly, people generally want to help if they can.

You may have noticed in the sample dialogues that you did not ask for a job. Asking for a job is pointless, because most of the time your contact will not have a job for you and it's the end of the conversation. When you ask for referrals concerning your target companies listed on your marketing plan, it opens up dialogue and future conversation. And believe me, if your contact does have an opening, he or she will most likely tell you about it.

When you finally connect with someone in one of your target companies, your goal is to identify the name of your next boss. If you were looking for a purchasing director job, you might say, "Who does the purchasing director report to in your company?" A follow-up question might be: "Does your company have a purchasing director?" Your goal is to bypass all the road blocks, including the human resources department. Human Resources do an excellent job in screening people out. Avoid HR at all costs unless you are actually seeking a position in human resources!

Once you finally get the name of the decision maker (your next boss) who can hire you, your phone strategy changes. Instead of asking him to provide you with referrals for your fifty target companies, you want to close him or her for a meeting. The dialogue might sound something like this:

Here's a sample dialogue when talking to a potential new boss:

You: "Hi, Mike. This is Ron Williams. Sarah Hillman referred me to you. Did I catch you at a bad time?"

Contact: "No, this is fine, how can I help?"

You: "Mike, I worked for five years as a purchasing director for XYZ company. Sarah suggested I try to get some face time with you. I was instrumental in launching a state-of-the-art inventory system and reduced their copier costs by 35 percent. I've done quite a bit of research on your company and someday I would like to be a part of your organization.

I would like to briefly meet with you so you can put a name with a face. Perhaps we can do breakfast, lunch, or I can stop by the office for a few minutes. What does your calendar look like in a couple of weeks?"

Of course, if you can get your referral to arrange a meeting with your potential next boss, then that will take the pressure off of you in making the phone call to close for a meeting. It will also put you in a stronger position, since you are being directly referred by someone your potential next boss already knows. That's powerful!

Key Points

1. Your marketing plan is the backbone of your job search campaign.

2. After you mount your mail campaign, use the phone to accelerate your job search in ways you cannot imagine.

3. You will need to make warm calls, at least ten per day or fifty per week.

4. Job hunting is a numbers game, and you need to keep the pipeline full.

5. Research your target companies and be flexible where you work.

6. Find and join groups or associations that your next boss may be a member of.

7. People will talk to you when you establish a bond of familiarity.

Thirteen

INTERVIEWING IS SELLING AND YOU ARE THE MERCHANDISE

"To do a really good interview, you have to be truly interested in the person."

- Daisy Fuentes

Charles Reade once said, "If you wish to please people, you must begin by understanding them." Take these words to heart. So far, you have learned about purpose, passion, preferences, talents, motivation, resumes, networking, and warm calls. You're heading in the right direction. You're on a journey to a place called work. However, how do you clinch the job offer? How do you land the job? Many are called. Few are chosen. Your objective now is to ace the interview and clinch the job.

Coca-Cola started up more than one hundred years ago in Atlanta. It was invented by a Confederate pharmacist named John Pemberton, and the original formula contained cocaine because it was used for medicine. In 1902, the company took out the cocaine and replaced it with coca leaves. Today, Coca-Cola generates over $30 billion in annual revenues. Why do people spend so much money on soft drinks?

I can answer that question with one word: marketing. Marketing gets people excited. Marketing motivates people to make decisions. And it's marketing that will motivate your interviewer to make you a job offer. With interviews, you are the product, as we discussed earlier with the Nixon campaign. You need to get the interviewer excited about you. Most of us will work about 8,500 days during our lifetime. Eighty percent of us will not get excited about our jobs; 20 percent will.

You need to get into the 20% group. You need to get excited about your interview and ultimately your job. Most interviewers are looking for the 20 percenters. The 20 percenters are not necessarily the best qualified for the job. However, they definitely are the best skilled in marketing themselves. I'm going to share with you ten great strategies for winning the interview and clinching the job offer. By the end of this chapter, you will learn how to make a great first impression. You'll find out what to do during the first two minutes of the interview. You'll learn how to add magic to your performance, how to speak the interviewer's language, and, finally, how to get the interviewer to like you. The interviewer, by the way, is your next boss. As mentioned earlier, you want to bypass human resources and talk directly with the decision maker.

1. Learn how to project a friendly attitude.

Your attitude can impact your behavior during an interview. It can have a profound impact on whether or not you get the job. If you are meeting with a potential next boss, that boss needs to like you. If he or she does not like you, you will not get hired. There has to be a good fit. The chemistry has to be right. What kind of attitude do you have? How do you come across when talking to strangers? Your attitude is a result of how you think. You are what you think. You think how you feel. You feel the way you act because action follows feelings. If you think you are confident, you will act with confidence. If you think like a winner, you'll act like a winner. If you think you are cheerful, you'll act like you're cheerful. Do you think interviewers want to hire confident, cheerful people? How do you generate a positive, cheerful attitude?

We previously discussed how you can instantly put yourself into a positive state of mind by using a technique called anchoring. Once you anchor that feeling, you activate it by pinching your left thumb with your right hand. Now feel that self-confidence and optimism during the interview. If you want to augment that feeling, think of a good joke or recall a funny story just before you go to the interview. Give yourself a good laugh. It will put you in a relaxed mood, and you'll feel less nervous. It is biochemically impossible to feel bad when you are laughing.

2. Make a good first impression.

Many interviewers do not know how to interview. Instead, they rely on gut instincts and attempt to size people up within the first two minutes. Many of us grew up in the school of first impressions. Birds of a feather flock together. The bigger they are, the harder they fall. It doesn't really matter that people are not birds and that some big men may be very light on their feet. There is nothing wrong in using gut instincts, but sometimes it is based on the interviewer's personality instead of your skills. What you say and do during the first two minutes is critical.

The first thing you need is a good posture. Would you hire someone that walks like he is down in the dumps and on his way to the gallows? You should have a brisk gait with stomach in and chest out. Yeah, just like the army. And if you don't think the receptionist is checking you out, think again.

Do you realize that if you stand up straight, put your shoulders back, take deep breaths, and look forward, you can't be depressed? The reason why you can't be depressed is because your brain is being told to be alert, vital, and resourceful. You need to have good posture.

What you wear is just as important as how you walk. You need to dress like a winner. When you go on an interview, wear a blue suit if you're a male and a blue dress or suit if you're a female. The color blue is the most popular color in the United States. Running second is dove gray, and third is hunter green. Be conservative. Don't wear ties that will give the interviewer a headache.

3. Wear a smile on your face.

How you walk and dress is obviously very important. However, the most important thing you wear is the smile on your face. You need to make your smile big. There are one hundred muscles in your face and eighteen different kinds of smiles. Use those muscles and raise those cheekbones. When you're smiling, the whole world smiles with you. There are some companies that make hiring decisions based on the number of times the applicant smiles.

You're about to meet the interviewer. Your posture is straight. You're dressed for success. Your smile is as big as you can make it. The next three things you need are good eye contact, high energy, and firm, moisture-free handshake. "Hi, I'm Joe Carroll. It's a pleasure to meet you." You need to generate energy, but don't storm in like the Incredible Hulk.

4. Show honest appreciation.

When is the last time someone expressed appreciation for something you did? Appreciation is something we all want, but never seem to get enough of. Interviewers are no exceptions. They want appreciation. When you show a little appreciation, the scales tilt in your favor. How do you show appreciation? Try saying this on your next initial meeting with an interviewer, "I really appreciate your taking the time to see me today."

5. Mirror the interviewer.

The best way to get the interviewer to like you is to mirror or match his or her actions. This technique is also known as pacing or aligning with the interviewer and is used by many successful sales people. How can you use words, tone, and body language to mirror the interviewer? Imitate his voice. Imitate his posture. Imitate his or her facial expressions and hand gestures. Just don't make it too obvious. Why is mirroring so effective? There are two reasons:

- People tend to hire people like themselves.

- Body language is the most effective communication device.

Seven percent of what is communicated is through words, 39 percent is by tone of voice, and 55 percent of all communications is a result of body language. Try to match the interviewer's language. Match his or her key words and phrases. For example, if the interviewer says, "In this company we try to cut corners." You might tell her at some point during the interview the following: "In my last position, I reduced costs by 20 percent by cutting corners, and this is how I did it."

People basically think in three different ways: seeing, hearing, and feeling. Your job is to figure out if the interviewer prefers words that see, hear, or feel. Use those same or similar words in your responses.

The interviewer that <u>sees</u> will say things like: "Let's keep things in perspective," "I see what you mean," "I can picture that," "Let me show you what I mean." The interviewer who prefers <u>hearing</u> will use auditory words: "I hear what you're saying," "That rings a bell," "Let me tell you more about my accomplishments," "Sounds good to me." Interviewers who use <u>feeling</u> words will say things like: "Let's touch base next week," "How do you feel about the job?" "I can handle that," "How does that grab you?" "Here's how I feel about what you just said." Again, what we're trying to do is imitate the interviewer and use words and phrases they tend to use because people hire people like themselves.

6. Ask a probing question.

Interviewers are more impressed with applicants that ask questions. They are less impressed with applicants who just sit there and answer questions. What you want to do is ask a question at the very beginning of the interview and before the interviewer starts asking you questions. If you ask the right question you can get information that will help you to answer the interviewer's questions. Here is the perfect question to ask: "What results are you looking for in this position over the next six months?" Once you have the answer to that question, you can adjust your answers to the interviewer's future questions.

7. Put some magic in your words.

There are three magical words that you absolutely must remember during every interview. These should be included in your major strengths, which you should be prepared to give examples of. The acronym for these three words is ERA, which stands for:

> **E**nergy
> **R**esponsibility
> **A**ccomplishment

The first magical word is "energy," and you better have plenty of it if you want that job. Emerson tells us that the world belongs to the energetic. So what do you say to the interviewer?

"Yes, Mr. Interviewer, one of my strongest qualities is energy. To help out with my family's expenses, I worked part-time at night and went to school during the day."

A high energy level suggests that you can do the job with enthusiasm. Companies don't want cars with dead batteries. They want cars that are charged up and ready to go!

The second magical word is "responsibility." Many people who get a job often lose it because of a lack of responsibility. If you don't have an alarm clock, buy one. If you can't give 100 percent, eight hours a day, don't apply for the job. For every one of you that can't give 100 percent, there are five others that can. Companies do not stay in business by paying a full week's salary for four days' worth of work. "Yes, Mr. Interviewer, I went through a twenty-two week training program, and I didn't miss one day." "Yes, Mr. Interviewer, when I start a job, I finish it. You can depend on it. My friends tell me I am very dependable."

The third magical word is "accomplishment." Why should I hire you? Can you make some concrete, factual statements that will give some idea regarding what you can do? "Mr. Interviewer, I saved my last company over $30,000 last year by developing a new inventory software program." "Mr. Interviewer, I have just completed a twenty-two week course in customer service, and I know how important it is to keep the customer happy." Remember this word, "accomplishment." It is better to be nobody who accomplishes something than somebody who accomplishes nothing.

There are also personal accomplishments that bridge the gap between the pulpit and the office. You should not hesitate to talk about some of these types of accomplishments with your interviewer. People want to hire good people. If you are doing some constructive work through church, synagogue, or charity, then it is something to talk about. "Mr. Interviewer, as a member of the Feed the Hungry program, I helped to feed three thousand needy families last year at a cost of $10 per person. The costs were kept down by my calling on companies and getting donations."

What does this say about you? You have a good heart. You are a communicator. You are numbers-oriented. You get things accomplished.

8. Never ask questions about benefits during the interview.

Remember, it's not what the employer can do for you. It's what you can do for your employer. Millions of people are out of work. Companies can pick and choose as they see fit. Your purpose is to bring value to the company, not to increase its expenses. You absolutely do not want to leave the interviewer with the impression that the only reason why you want the job is because of the benefits program the company may have in place.

9. Make a good last impression.

Big smile. Direct eye contact. "Mr. Interviewer, I believe I have the qualifications you are looking for. It sounds like a great opportunity. I look forward to hearing from you soon." End with a firm, moisture-free handshake.

Send a handwritten thank you note on quality stationery. Most of your competitors will not send a thank-you note. If you do, it helps tilt the scales in your favor. The note should be brief and enthusiastic. Reiterate your major accomplishments. End on a positive note. Make sure there are no spelling or grammar errors. Always carry a miniature dictionary with you. Even people like Dan Quayle, the former vice president of the United States, make spelling errors.

10. Never give up.

You will be going on many interviews throughout your career. You may hear a lot of noes before you finally get to a yes. By accelerating the number of noes, you will get to yes faster. Never consider no a personal rejection. People who are successful never allow rejection or the fear of failure to get in their way. Here is one example of someone who never allowed rejection to get in the way.

The person failed in business at the age of twenty-one. He was defeated in a legislative race at age twenty-three. He failed again in business at age twenty-four. He overcame the death of his sweetheart at age twenty-six. He had a nervous breakdown at age twenty-seven. He lost a congressional race at age thirty-four. He lost a congressional race at age thirty-six. He lost a senatorial race at age forty-five. He failed in an effort to become vice president at age forty-seven. He lost a senatorial race at age forty-nine. He was elected president of the United States at age forty-nine. His name was Abraham Lincoln. Never, never, never give up!

Key Points

1. It's all about marketing and getting the interviewer excited about you.

2. Learn how to project a friendly attitude.

3. Make a good first impression.

4. Wear a smile on your face.

5. Show honest appreciation.

6. Mirror the interviewer.

7. Remember the three magical words: energy, responsibility, and accomplishment.

8. Never ask questions about benefits during the interview.

9. Make a good last impression.

10. Never give up.

Fourteen

HOW TO CLEAN YOUR LIFE WITH A NEW BROOM

"Twenty years from now you will be more disappointed by the things you didn't do than by the ones you did do. So throw off the bowlines. Sail away from the safe harbor. Catch the trade winds in your sails. Explore. Dream. Discover."

- Mark Twain

What in the world do tolerations have to do with a job search? What exactly do we mean by tolerations? I look at tolerations as job interference. It's those little things that get in the way of performing well in front of some recruiter. You need to be on your game in job searches. Tolerations take you off your game. Did you ever get a headache? According to a Louis Harris survey, 73 percent of all Americans suffer from occasional headaches. Tolerations, I believe, are one cause of headaches.

Tolerations are things that we allow or endure. We put up with things in life and look at them as a mild inconvenience regardless of the consequences. In Charles Dickens's *A Christmas Carol*, Scrooge felt it was a piece of cheese that was causing his apparitions and simply viewed the ghost as a mere form of mild indigestion. We tolerate people at work we don't like because we depend on the income derived from the job and we don't want to jeopardize our security. We tolerate certain relatives simply because it is politically correct and we don't want to offend anyone and start a blood feud. We tolerate certain neighbors because we live in the same neighborhood and need to get along and don't want to upset the apple cart. We ignore the clutter in our homes because we have other, more important priorities. We keep things that we have not looked at in years simply because we're afraid we might need them someday, or perhaps we can sell them on eBay in ten years and make a profit. Tolerations may even be viewed as ways to avoid confrontation, arguments, and headaches. I can't be bothered, you might say. I have other things to worry about. How about removing the word "worry" from your vocabulary?

These words may assume that I am addressing the middle class, homeowners, and even wealthy Americans. I'm sorry to say that even people that are living by their bootstraps do not get a free ride. Many people without money carry around their bags of tolerations. Tolerations do not distinguish between the rich and the poor. Regardless of your station in life, you are dragging and enduring your tolerations hour by hour, day by day, and year by year. Isn't it about time to get rid of these burdens like they're sitting on the back of a tired, old horse?

The problem with tolerations is they are very deceptive. They often appear to be insignificant. They're viewed as a mild annoyance and we simply shut them out of our minds. Sometimes we think it's the Christian thing to do. Did the many wives of King Henry VIII tolerate him at least until their heads were cut off? Did the hundreds of followers of Jim Jones follow his madness until they were finally forced to commit suicide? Tolerations can have consequences. They can rob you of your energy, vitality, and strength. They can get in the way of your achieving happiness in life. Over time, they can even be life-threatening.

To dwell on our purpose, follow our passions and use our talents requires a clear head. We can't be having a lot of junk inside our minds that hampers our thinking and ultimately what we want to achieve in life. Eliminating tolerations from your life will be like drinking a health tonic. It will enable you to focus on the important things. It will get rid of the clutter in your mind and you will feel better. Eliminating tolerations may not seem like a big deal for you. After all, you have survived all of these years with your tolerations and you seem to be functioning just fine. However, the problem with tolerations is that they tend to nag at you in the recesses of your mind. You may decide to put things off simply because you can get to it tomorrow. This delay and avoidance mentality is a recipe for stress and ulcers. Over a period of many years, these annoyances can leap from a mere seed to a giant thorn bush.

In fact, one of the leading six causes of death in the United States is due to stress. When you start on a program to remove your tolerations, your stress levels will go down and your mental energy will go up. By the way, meditation is a great way to relax, improve concentration, and communicate with your inner voice. Jeremy Taylor once said, "Meditation is the tongue of the soul and the language of our spirit." Practicing meditation has many benefits.

But meditation alone will not get rid of your tolerations. So how do you get rid of your tolerations? You start by making lists of everything you are currently tolerating and, as you eliminate your tolerations, cross them off your list. Write them down and cross them off. Your list will include all tolerations from big to small. I suggest you categorize your list by categories such as house, work, relationships, habits, worries, health, and your financial situation.

Most people hate to throw stuff away, especially after they spent a bundle to buy it. According to the Self Storage Association, the industry trade group for the owners of self-storage businesses, Americans have over two billion square feet of self-storage in about fifty thousand facilities throughout the United States that are generating over $20 billion a year in revenues. We're actually willing to spend money to save our stuff. How about just stop buying stuff and getting rid of the stuff you don't need?

One of my worst tolerations was putting up with clutter in the house. Then one day I decided that I wanted to get rid of all the junk that was a total waste of space. I took the first opportunity when I moved. I rented a fourteen-foot metal container and filled it up completely three times! I had a real sense of accomplishment. After I moved, I did it again. I felt refreshed and free with a tremendous sense of freedom. I also freed up a lot of space.

What about that neighbor you don't like? The Hatfields and McCoys have never quite figured it out, although I think the passage of time has healed most of their disputes. You do have options. If things are that bad, you can always move. You might try to make peace, but you're probably better off going with your gut instincts. Avoidance may be your only option when it comes to a rude neighbor.

Becoming aware of your tolerations is a tremendous step forward. Once you realize what is keeping you up at night, solutions will start to unfold in the morning. Yet this is no easy task. You may literally have hundreds of tolerations once you stop and think about it.

To get the ball rolling right now, put this book down and take some time to think of a toleration you are putting up with at home or in the office. Now develop an action plan to eliminate it. Just do it. Make it happen. Congratulations! Life will never be the same for you again.

Key Points

1. Tolerations are things we allow or endure.

2. Eliminating tolerations from your life will be like drinking a health tonic.

3. Becoming aware of your tolerations is the first step to eliminating them.

Fifteen

TRUST YOUR HUNCHES AND GO WITH YOUR INSTINCTS

"You have first an instinct, then an opinion, then a knowledge, as the plant has root, bud, and fruit. Trust the instinct to the end, though you can render no reason."

- Ralph Waldo Emerson

If I were to take a survey of workers, probably 10% would say they love their job. Another 10% would say they hate their job, and everyone else is somewhere in between. For many of us, the job was simply the end result of a help-wanted ad on Sunday morning over coffee and bagels. For many of us, work is simply a means to an end. Part of the strategy in achieving great outcomes in life is to follow your instincts. Ralph Waldo Emerson once said, "Trust your instincts to the end, though you can render no reason." You need to listen to your inner voice. Trust your hunches. Go with your sixth sense. Our instincts were our first built-in survival kit long before written communications, designer jeans, and city skyscrapers. Before we gained knowledge and advanced intellect, we had to go with our instincts. That's all we had. When you are considering a job offer within those first ninety days, trust your gut when making decisions. Your instincts will serve you well. Of course you want to lean on the side of caution. Allow your rational mind to weigh in on your instincts. Give it some thought, but lean heavily on your instincts.

All of us, at one time or another, have experienced intuition firsthand. We have heard many of the expressions and may have uttered some of them ourselves, such as, "I have a funny feeling about this"; "I have a hunch"; "a little bird told me"; "my gut instinct tells me." Yet, science and philosophers have argued for years over the validity of intuition. "Instinct" is defined as a natural or innate impulse, inclination, or aptitude and a natural intuitive power. I believe instincts are a gift. They're built into our DNA. They are a communication warp hole to our soul. I also believe that we have not yet learned how to fully harness the power of our instincts, just as we have not fully harnessed the power of our mind. Albert Einstein once said that we use only 10 percent of our brain power. After all, we've only been around here for about three hundred thousand years or so. Combining intuition with experience can be very powerful. When mankind learns to harness the full power of its brain, we will make progress that will shatter all possibilities.

There are some scientists and psychologists who have studied intuition and clearly believe in the power of going with your gut. Gerd Gigerenzer is a German psychologist and director at the Max Planck Institute for Human Development. He tells us that gut feelings are quick in consciousness and can outperform optimization techniques because they exploit our mental capacities and environmental structures. Ken Paller, professor of psychology at Northwestern University, conducted a study that concluded quick decisions were superior to those who had more time to think about it.

Instincts have impacted our decisions from the beginning of the written word. Instincts caused the Three Wise Men, known as the Magi, to take another route home instead of returning to King Herod and facing potential danger. Joseph and Mary fled Bethlehem with the infant Jesus after Joseph was warned in a dream that it was unsafe for them to remain there. Indeed, all of the prophets who have come down to us through the ages were divinely inspired with ideas from God. Were they following their instincts?

Some of the most daring and successful decisions in life are often based on sheer instincts. Sergeant Alvin York was drafted into the Army in 1917 during World War I. Although he struggled with the thought of killing other human beings, his survival instincts and the safety of his fellow soldiers took over in the heat of a battle. During the battle of the Argonne Forest in 1918, he killed twenty-five Germans, destroyed thirty-five machines guns, and captured 132 prisoners almost single-handedly. He did not have time to plan his strategy out. He used a combination of his expert marksmanship and his gut instincts to win the battle. He subsequently received the French Medaille Militaire and Croix de Guerre, the Italian Groce de Guerra and the American Medal of Honor.

Most human resource professionals will advise you not to use your gut instincts when making hiring decisions for fear of making biased decisions. A biased decision cannot be defended in a court of law. However, the use of behavioral or pattern interview questionnaires helps recruiters to defend their decisions based on reason and logic. However, most recruiters also know that these questionnaires do not always result in great hires. If you combine them with your gut instincts, you are in a much better position to make the right decision.

Once again, we find that we do not have all the answers to the universe. Intuition is certainly a big question mark out there. Nevertheless, I urge you to go with your sixth sense. Albert Einstein once said, "The intuitive mind is a sacred gift and the rational mind is a faithful servant. We have created a society that honors the servant and has forgotten the gift." Einstein knew what he was talking about. When he discovered the theory of relativity, it was not during intense, rational thinking in the science laboratory. He was actually playing with his grandson, blowing bubbles. The answer to the theory of relativity occurred to him when one of those bubbles drifted off in the air. It somehow put his mind in focus, and he suddenly realized the answer. It was an emotional power shift. Yes, miracles and breakthroughs can happen in the twinkling of an eye. The point is that your instincts and the right answers will often kick in when you least expect it.

Key Points

1. Our instincts were our first built-in survival kit long before written communications, designer jeans, and city skyscrapers.

2. Combining intuition with experience can be very powerful.

3. Many scientists and psychologists have studied intuition and clearly believe in the power of going with your gut.

4. Trust your gut when considering job offers from employers.

Sixteen

YOUR BLUEPRINT FOR LIFE REQUIRES A FEW GOALS

"Goals are dreams with deadlines."

- Diana Scharf Hunt

By now you have certainly nailed down your passion statement. You are keenly aware of your purpose, preferences, and talents. You made the connection and aligned your purpose and talents with your job target. You have developed a new appreciation for compassion. To get your dream job in ninety days or less requires some goals and action steps. The failure to establish goals and action steps is one of the leading reasons why coaches are in such hot demand these days. Most coaches hold you accountable for developing and achieving your goals.

Why is it that some people are very successful in life where others fail? Why are some wealthy, yet lack a sense of fulfillment and happiness? Sometimes our talents and passions cause us to be happy or successful in one area of life, but we fail miserably in other areas of our life. It's really important to bring it all together. To maximize your full potential, we need to explore the following key questions in life:

1. Are your passions, talents, and preferences properly aligned with the work that you do?

2. Have you established goals that will impact your financial needs?

3. Have you developed a career plan that will ensure long-term success?

4. Have you put a process in place to ensure the health and vitality of yourself and your family?

5. Do you have a plan to help others who are perhaps less fortunate than you?

6. Are you clear on aligning your passion, purpose, talents, and preferences in life with your chosen profession?

7. Are you committed to achieving self-fulfillment?

For those who believe in an inner voice, we start with our passions and talents. This is the core of being human. I don't want to discount preferences, which impact all of our major decisions. For example, if you prefer attaining wealth, chances are you would object to working for a company that is nonprofit. If you enjoy autonomy, you will not like working for a micromanager. If you are passionate about protecting the earth from the excesses of man, chances are you will not be working for a company that poisons the earth's air.

Preferences often surface through your gut instincts. Deep down inside, you will know if something is right or wrong for you, and that will guide your decision. However, it is important for you to know your passions and talents, because they will become a huge part of your success in life. Since you already developed your passion statement, you should already have a good idea if you are in the right field or not. If not, go back and develop your passion statement.

Goals are really important, yet they are one of our weakest areas when it comes time for execution. The mind is willing, but the body is weak. Earl Nightingale provides us with some really good advice about goals: "The more intensely we feel about an idea or a goal, the more assuredly the idea, buried deep in our subconscious, will direct us along the path to its fulfillment."

The classic example is New Year's Eve resolutions. We make a list of all the things we want to accomplish in the next year, and what happens? Most of us fail miserably. Temptation knocks and we open the door with welcoming arms. According to a survey of three thousand people conducted by the British psychologist Richard Wiseman, 88 percent of all resolutions fail! How did the remaining 12 percent succeed?

We can start to learn the answers by adopting some of the principles in this book. I suspect the people in the 12 percent group got more rest. Part of the problem may sound like an oversimplification. Our brains get tired. Tired brains do not make good decisions, and they become casualties of temptation. Sorry—it's due to mankind's limited time on earth. We have not yet harnessed the energy to maximize the use of our brains. Bigger brains make better decisions. We have all heard the adage: Let's sleep on it. That adage makes perfectly good sense when it is reinforced by scientific data.

In several experiments and field studies by University of Minnesota psychologist Kathleen Vohs, making multiple decisions fatigues the brain and we wind up making poor choices. You can't have too many cooks in the same kitchen. Things get burnt out and bent out of shape. There is a lot of merit to focusing on one thing at a time. Did you ever notice when your office is neat and not cluttered, you can actually think better? Try it sometime. Peter Drucker, the management guru, once said, "Concentration is the key to economic results. No other principles of effectiveness are violated as constantly today as the basic principle of concentration."

Perhaps there is some merit in taking a siesta in the afternoon or a catnap in the office. You do need to get the proper amount of sleep. Most experts say you should be getting between seven and eight hours of sleep a night. Of course, there are those macho men who boast they can get by on four to five hours of sleep. Their batteries will not last very long. The odds are against it. The problem or challenge that we currently have is with our brains. On the evolutionary scale, our brains are still in the early formative stages of development. Yes, mankind has accomplished great things, but we have a long way to go.

We are still carrying around our appendix, for example, which is no longer a functional part of our anatomy. It is believed by many that the appendix lost its original function. According to Charles Darwin, it was once used to digest leaves. Others argue that it was another intestine designed to store extra food, since we did not get three square meals a day when we were running around with the Neanderthals. When we had food, we ate more since we did not know when the next meal was coming. The point is that human evolution did not occur overnight. Who knows? In ten thousand years, mental telepathy could be the preferred method of communication and drive the phone companies out of business or into a new business. Instead of applauding a speaker, the audience transmits mental appreciation waves to the speaker, causing the speaker to slightly levitate in the air. Sounds far fetched, but who knows. Did the Roman Empire ever conceive of planes, trains, or automobiles?

Today, we need to compensate for a brain that weighs less than the brain of a sperm whale or an Asian elephant and operates at roughly 10 percent of its capacity. The human brain is highly complex and weighs 1,500 grams. The average skull holds a brain of about 1,400 cubic centimeters. This is huge in comparison to the size of our body. Our brain size is roughly twice the size of early *Homo erectus* who lived in Africa over one million years ago. Big brains require a lot of energy. Roughly, 20 percent of our metabolism is devoted to brain function, which is a huge amount of energy. According to Daniel Drubach in *The Brain Explained* (Prentice-Hall, 2000), "Although the brain accounts for less than 2 percent of a person's weight, it consumes 20 percent of the body's energy." If you cut a person's energy off for ten minutes, you risk permanent brain damage.

There is scientific evidence that we can actually increase the energy our brains require. According to research at the Human Cognitive Neuroscience Unit of the University of Northumbria, a single dose of the herbal extract ginkgo improves blood flow, oxygenation, and glucose metabolism. Similar results occur when we consume glucose or ginkgo combined with ginseng. Research has also proven that consuming foods high in glucose content actually improve short-term memory and cognitive performance. Glucose is a form of sugar produced when carbohydrates are digested. The best sources of carbohydrates include vegetables, fruit, and high fiber. Bad carbohydrates should, of course, be avoided, such as cake, candy, and other products high in sugar content.

In addition to tired and overworked brains, the other problem is a lack of focus or awareness of the problem. This is why writing your goals are so important. The brain forgets 80 percent of detail within twenty-four hours and 99 percent within two weeks. Writing things down helps the brain remember and what to focus on. I once read about a Harvard MBA study about students and goals. Three percent of the students had written goals. Thirteen percent had goals, but not in writing, and 84 percent had no goals. Ten years later they interviewed the same students. The 13 percent with unwritten goals earned twice as much as those with no goals. The 3 percent with written goals earned, on average, ten times more than the other 97 percent combined! Don't you think it's a good idea to write down your goals? If you don't write them down, you run the risk of not getting them done. Getting things done typically puts you in the 12 percent group.

When you start to develop your goals, you need to cover all the bases. Many of us have heard of the acronym SMART goals. It stands for specific, measureable, achievable, realistic, and timely. This is a timeless acronym and still makes a great deal of sense today. All of your goals should have these guidelines built into them. The brain does not like fuzzy stuff. The more specific you can be about your goal, the easier it will be for the brain to process your request and make it happen. Here are some examples of well-stated goals:

1. I will obtain a new job in ninety days or less.

2. I will pay off all of my credit cards by October 1.

3. I will be an outstanding farmer and till the land within six months.

4. I will lose ten pounds within four months by working out every day for thirty minutes and maintaining a 1,800 daily calorie diet.

5. I will provide my family with undivided attention and quality time on a regular basis.

When writing goals, try to expand your horizons and create stretch goals. In the early part of my career, I was a speechwriter and training director in the insurance industry. One day, I decided that I wanted to be a human resources director. So I applied for an HR director's position for a facilities management company. Naïve? Perhaps. Bold? No question about it. When asked do you have any experience in HR, I said, "No, but, I've taken some HR management courses in college." I got the job for two reasons. Experience had nothing to do with it. They liked me, and I was a certified trainer. Part of your strategy is to decide what you want and then pursue it with passion. There's nothing you can't do once you set your mind to it.

The last goal that you need to focus on is helping others. There was a great story I once read about a farmer named Fleming. It is told below:

> His name was Fleming, and he was a poor Scottish farmer. One day, while trying to make a living for his family, he heard a cry for help coming from a nearby bog. He dropped his tools and ran to the bog.
>
> There, mired to his waist in black muck, was a terrified boy, screaming and struggling to free himself. Farmer Fleming saved the lad from what could have been a slow and terrifying death.
>
> The next day, a fancy carriage pulled up to the Scotsman's sparse surroundings. An elegantly dressed nobleman stepped out and introduced himself as the father of the boy Farmer Fleming had saved.
>
> "I want to repay you," said the nobleman. "You saved my son's life."
>
> "No, I can't accept payment for what I did," the Scottish farmer replied waving off the offer. At that moment, the farmer's own son came to the door of the family hovel.
>
> "Is that your son?" the nobleman asked.

Your Blueprint For Life Requires A Few Goals

"Yes," the farmer replied proudly.

"I'll make you a deal. Let me provide him with the level of education my own son will enjoy. If the lad is anything like his father, he'll no doubt grow to be a man we both will be proud of." And that he did.

Farmer Fleming's son attended the very best schools and in time, graduated from St. Mary's Hospital Medical School in London, and went on to become known throughout the world as the noted Sir Alexander Fleming, the discoverer of penicillin.

Years afterward, the same nobleman's son who was saved from the bog was stricken with pneumonia.

What saved his life this time? Penicillin.

The name of the nobleman? Lord Randolph Churchill. His son's name?

Sir Winston Churchill.

Someone once said: What goes around comes around.

Work like you don't need the money.

Love like you've never been hurt.

Dance like nobody's watching.

Sing like nobody's listening.

Live like it's heaven on earth.

Zig Ziglar once said: "You can have everything you want in life, just as long as you help enough other people get what they want in life." Proverbs such as these are also related to some of the universal laws that have existed for centuries. Just imagine what the advanced and enlightened mind would be like ten thousand years from now. In an advanced civilization, there would be no war, crime, famine, hunger, or atrocities. Our animal instincts and the hunter that dwells in all of us would be totally removed from our genetic makeup. Our species would have evolved to a higher place.

Our challenge is to try and capture the essence of that future in our hearts and minds today. Think of your future possibilities if time, money and station in life were not roadblocks.

What would you have to do today to be happy and successful upon retirement?

If you were to fast-forward to the end of your time on earth, what would people say about you? All the motivation in the world will not move you to become the person you want to be. You need to search your heart and find the answers. You are in control. Your destiny must come from within. Your future is up to you working in harmony with your passions, preferences and talents. Strive to fulfill all of your dreams, hopes, and goals by living a passionate and compassionate life.

ABOUT THE AUTHOR

Joe Carroll is vice-president of human resources for IST Management Services. He is also a career coach, author and international speaker.

He is member of the International Coach Federation and the Association of Career Professionals International. He was appointed Fellow Practitioner by the Institute of Career Certification International. He is also certified as a senior professional in human resources by the Society for Human Resource Management.

Joe has published numerous articles on recruiting and career management in magazines such as the *Facility Management Journal*, *Business To Business*, *Workforce*, *Legal Management*, and *Human Resource Information Management*.

Joe earned his bachelor's degree in English from Queens College and his MBA from the College of Insurance in New York City.

If you are interested in engaging Joe Carroll as either a career coach or speaker, go to his Web site for more information or send an e-mail to:

Joekane @aol.com.

www.career-coach-now.com

Made in the USA
Lexington, KY
20 January 2012